Lost Restaurants OF TUCSON

Rita Connelly

AMERICAN PALATE

Published by American Palate
A Division of The History Press
Charleston, SC
www.historypress.net

Cover images: "Ronquillo's Bakery," Walter L. Goodwin Jr., 1965. *Commissioned by the Tucson Art Center. From the collection of the Tucson Museum of Art and Historic Block*; Big Boot. *Courtesy Drew and Kandie Vactor*; Neon Cactus. *Courtesy author's collection*; Elysian Grove Market. *Courtesy Library of Congress*; Richilieu restaurant. *Courtesy Arizona Historical Society*; Mexican food. *Courtesy Creative Commons.*

First published 2015

Manufactured in the United States

ISBN 978.1.46711.885.9

Library of Congress Control Number: 2015914237

Notice: The information in this book is true and complete to the best of our knowledge. It is offered without guarantee on the part of the author or The History Press. The author and The History Press disclaim all liability in connection with the use of this book.

This book is dedicated to my husband, John Connelly, for his patience, driving skills, support and love. So many of the meals and memories would be nothing without you.

And to Riene Connelly Gelman, for being a wonderful daughter and a great front-of-the-house person and for teaching me so much about food. Like your dad, none of this would've been possible without sharing so many meals with you.

For Sam Gelman, a great chef and a great son-in-law.

For Charlie Gelman, my sweet grandson, for all the meals to come.

Contents

Acknowledgements

Megan Laddusaw, my commissioning editor, for her help and support. Also, Ryan Finn, my copyeditor, whose patience knew no bounds. Thanks to the marketing team at The History Press.

Susan Dolan, registrar and collections manager at Tucson Museum of Art, for her help obtaining photos and for all the good meals we shared.

Becky Cowan for answering my shout out for restaurant memorabilia.

Karyn Zoldan and Edie Jarolim for their support and insight.

Norma Gentry for her many connections.

Jimmy Boegle, my editor at the *Tucson Weekly*, who gave me the job of a lifetime and went along with my idea to feature "Sorely Missed Restaurants" in that paper.

Drew and Kandie Vactor for The Tack Room story and great images.

Janos Wilder for his fabulous food over the years, his stories and his help with photos.

ACKNOWLEDGEMENTS

The Gekas family—Kiki Kinkade, Jimmy Gekas and Genie Patterson—for their family stories, the menus and the connection to Gus Lettas, as well as lunch. Chuck Hamm also had some great stories about his time as a busboy there.

Jim Murphy, Jeff Azersky and Marianne Baines for their collective and individual stories about so many restaurants.

Ellen Burke Van Slyke for taking time out of her busy day and for hiring my daughter many years ago.

Doug Levy for his history and loan of a book of restaurant menus.

Jonathan Landeen, who had information about both Charles and the Solarium and Restaurant Row.

Kim Moran for the stories about her mom and aunts and their Three Sisters Vietnamese restaurant.

Danny Scordato for clearing up the facts.

Alice Mezon and Bryan Mezon for telling me stories of their family and the role it played in both Tucson's history and the culinary scene.

Marguerite Brown and Julie Valenzuela, who were some of my earliest interviewees, and for the cool pictures of Gordo.

Pina Colosimo for seeing me again, the photos and the tiramisu (it was fabulous).

Vince, Assunta and Joe Ali for the beautiful menus, photos and family history.

Matt Russell for promoting me and for all the cool stories about "the Steer."

Frank Powers for the great photos of the Grill and Karlen Ross, who managed the Grill. Their input was perfect.

Benny Benedetto for being the best waiter in Tucson and the inside scoop about the Olive Tree.

ACKNOWLEDGEMENTS

Michael Veres for notes on Daniel's—both of them.

Ryan Clark for his insights on his mentor and friend, Alan Zeman.

Alan Zeman for so many contacts and insights, as well as a nosh.

Steve Marshall for the photos and information and for bringing my husband, John, and me together.

Dr. Patricia Sparks for those photos I really needed and Dr. Jennifer Muir Bowers for the connection to Penelope's.

Dr. Jim Griffith for his stories.

Michelle Araneta and Ginger and Michael Master for reminding me how wonderful their parents were.

Fran Markowitz, a total stranger but new friend, for connecting me to Michael Veres and Jolie Siebert for being a great connection.

Jack Tate and Ralph Avella for their kitchen memories.

Tim Fuller for the beautiful photo of Janos Wilder, even though the photo didn't get used.

Rocco DiGrazia of Rocco's Little Chicago for coming into work right after vacation to let me take a photo.

My brother, Stan Postorino, for chatting up a complete stranger in the airport in London, which led to meeting Andrea Davis, that stranger, who gave suggestions and info on the Carousel Gardens and a connection to Jerry's Ming House. Thanks, Andrea.

My sister, Nancy Postorino Reeves, for many years of support.

Joe Abi-Ad for the stories of Le Mediterranean.

Danny Lee for Chinese history, international, national and local.

ACKNOWLEDGEMENTS

The team at Arizona Historical Society for their patience and willingness to help me with a million requests, especially Lizeth Zepeda and Caitlin Lampman.

The librarians at Pima County Library.

The librarians at University of Arizona Library Special Collections.

Dwight and Christy Schannep of the American Antique Mall for sharing their collection of postcards and the technical help to save them.

To my friends who contributed their townie knowledge about all those little lost places: Don and Libby Mack, Barry and Susan Frank, Bobby Moreno and Joe and Pam Pierce.

And to all the strangers I met along the way who, once they found out I was writing this book, contributed information just because.

Introduction

TUCSON'S TABLES, TUCSON'S TASTES

The history of the lost restaurants of Tucson has as much to do with the people as it does the places. The Gekas and Scordato families ran restaurants for decades. Chefs Janos Wilder, Donna Nordin and Alan Zeman were at the forefront of the New Southwestern cuisine. Larry Colligan of the Hidden Valley Inn and Diego A. Valenzuela of Gordo's Mexicateria & Mexicatessen became local celebrities due to their television commercials and snappy catchphrases. And over time, a strong bond grew among the owners, chefs and diners.

I spoke to many people to help gather information about the restaurants that are included in this book. Every person I spoke with had their favorites, and all were eager to share. As they started talking, a certain look would come across their faces. They'd lean in, and you could hear the excitement in their voices. And everyone had a story to tell.

People met their future spouses at this restaurant or got engaged at that restaurant. They celebrated a birth, a graduation or a job promotion at their special spot. A delicious dish was recalled. Names of favorite servers brought smiles to their faces. There were plenty of work-related stories, as well. I was amazed and grateful by the variety and passion.

But the list kept getting longer and longer. I was concerned as to how to narrow the names down. Eventually, a pattern emerged. Certain restaurants kept popping up: The Tack Room, the Palomino, the Solarium, Johnie's, the Hidden Valley Inn, Janos and more. The book started to come into focus.

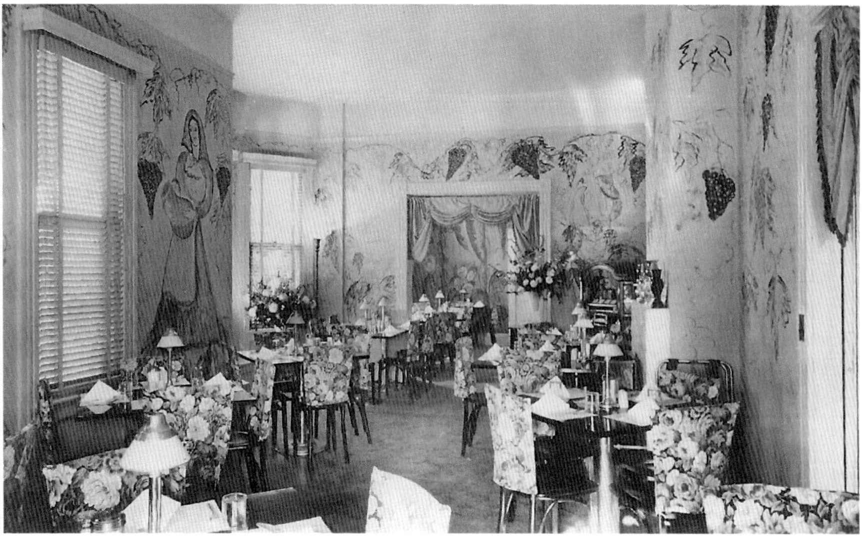

Napoli, faded into oblivion. *From the collection of Dwight and Christy Schannep, American Antique Mall.*

Still, a word of apology to the places and people I didn't include. Places like Cuvee, the Presidio Grill, the Frontier Drive-in, Red Sky, Le Bistro and more were all great places that people loved, but time and space were limited. I apologize to the restaurant staff and to all their fans.

Sadly, too, some of the favorite restaurants are truly lost. Andy's came up more than once, but information on the place was impossible to find. The only reminders of the Original Mexican and Italian Restaurant that opened downtown in 1927 was a postcard for sale on the Internet and a few advertisements in old Tucson visitor guidebooks. In some cases, when that happened, I relied only on peoples' memories.

It also should be noted that I worked at several of the restaurants featured in this book. I was a server at Ports O'Call when I first moved to town. I was also a server at Araneta's Mexico Inn on and off for several years. And I slung pizzas and poured beer at the Last Chance Pizza Mill. (It's where I met my husband.) With these restaurants, my memories certainly are a part their stories.

Every restaurant in this book has a story. I hope it does them justice.

Chapter 1

A Little History Before We Start

The staff of El Charro Mexican restaurant (still going strong as of publication date) was standing in the parking lot across from the restaurant watching fireworks fill the sky from atop of A Mountain. Tucson was celebrating its 200th birthday. The date was August 20, 1975, almost a full year before America's bicentennial.[1] Tucsonans are proud that they live in one of the oldest cities in the United States.

Native peoples occupied the Tucson valley as early as 800 BC, and Spanish padres, most notably Padre Kino, built missions in the area for decades.[2] Near what was to become Tucson, his followers built San Xavier del Bac, a tall, eye-catching church that sits on the Tohono O'odham Indian Reservation.[3] Kino brought cattle and wheat to the area, which, as time moved along, became central to the diets of Tucsonans. But it wasn't until 1775 that the Presidio de Tucson was established in the name of Spain by Lieutenant Colonel Hugo O'Conor. It took another seven years to build walls that were high enough for protection against the Apaches. And even then, raids lasted well into the 1800s. Life in the pueblo was difficult but simple, and certainly there were no public dining rooms.

Surrounded by mountain ranges (the Santa Catalinas to the near north, the Rincons to the east, the Tucson and Tortolitas to the west and the Santa Ritas to the far south), the area holds unprecedented beauty. The skies seemed eternally blue, the spaces were wide and plush and it was in many ways a perfect stop between the eastern cities and the Pacific Ocean.

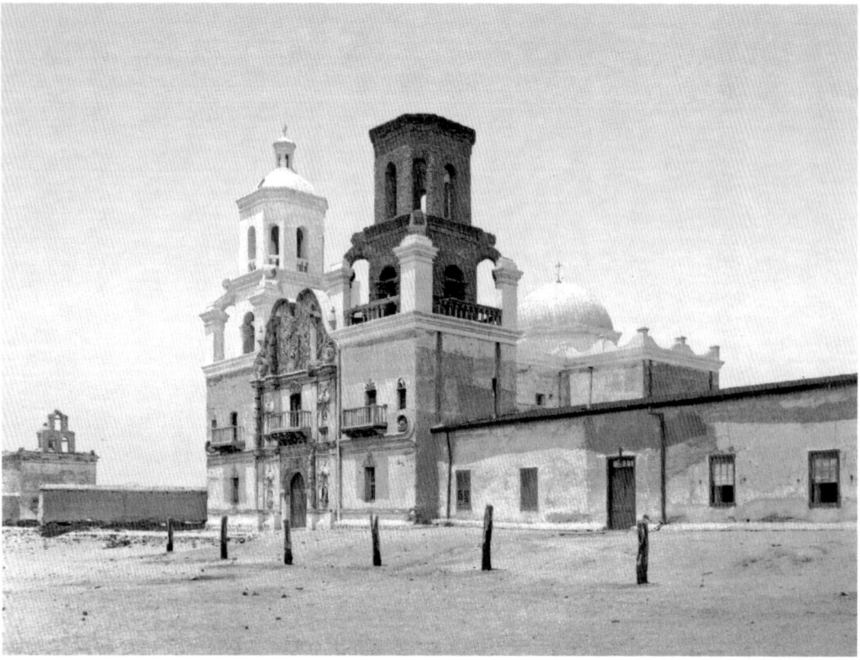

San Xavier Mission in earlier days. *Library of Congress.*

Over time, Tucson would live under the Spanish flag, the Mexican flag, the Confederate flag and the flag of the United States of America. In 1912, Arizona became a state, and one more flag flew over Tucson. During that time, Tucson grew from a village of 915 citizens (1860) to a city of 20,292 (1920).[4]

The Gadsden Purchase of 1854 made the southern section of Arizona and New Mexico part of the United States. Being a territory came with some rules and regulations that required property owners to register their home and businesses. An official map of the city was also created. All this attracted more and more people to the area.[5] The Confederate troops only stayed about six months, and once they left, stability took hold and people began to arrive in greater numbers.

Needless to say, early settlers were a mixed bag. People came for adventure. Some came for their health as Tucson became known a haven for tuberculosis sufferers. Land speculators came looking to strike it rich. Hardscrabble types hoped to find gold, silver and other minerals in them there hills. Veterans of the Civil War came to start over. Others who were just passing through liked what they saw and decided to stay.

A LITTLE HISTORY BEFORE WE START

Tucson has always been a city that embraced multiculturalism. Not that prejudice and discrimination didn't exist, but minorities owned businesses, many of which were restaurants. Two Native American nations had roots in the area: the Tohono O'odham and the Pasqua Yaqui. In 1874, President Grant established the San Xavier Indian Reservation on the land occupied by the O'odham Nation. Relations with these tribes were peaceful but exclusionary. No doubt lives crossed, but not on the level of other "minorities."

Neighborhoods were segregated. The original Chinatown was located west of the main business area. Other Chinatowns followed as each one was torn down in the name of progress.[6] Certain neighborhoods didn't allow African Americans to live in them, and there were several small pockets that were exclusively African American.[7]

Because Tucson was once part of Mexico, many Mexican families had established roots in the city. Some of them had become quite wealthy and were prominent members of the community. But they were in the minority. Mexicans did have their own neighborhoods, but mixed marriages blurred these lines a bit. Although there are no hard records showing any Mexican restaurants, Mexican food was daily fare. Neal Carmody wrote in his book

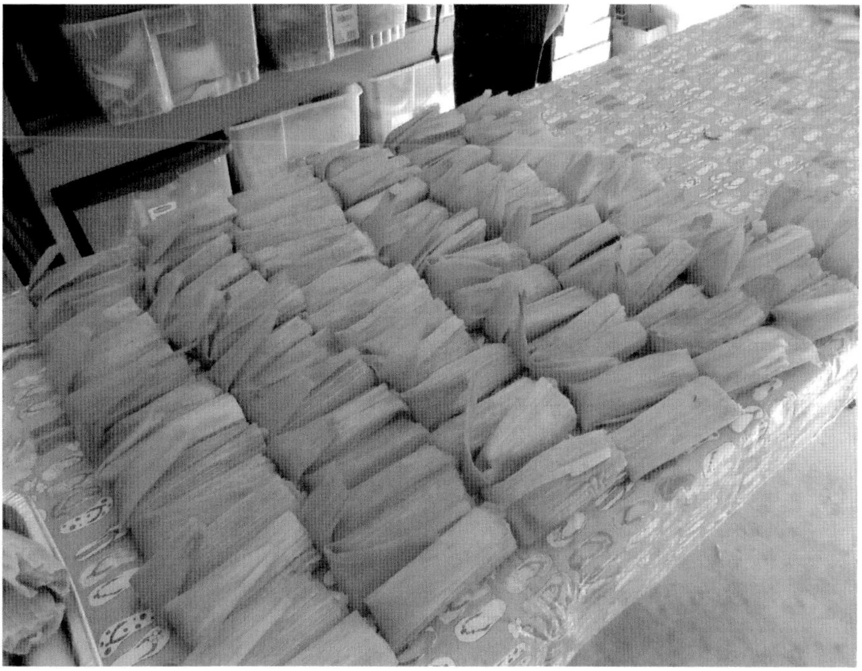

Tamales. *Author's collection.*

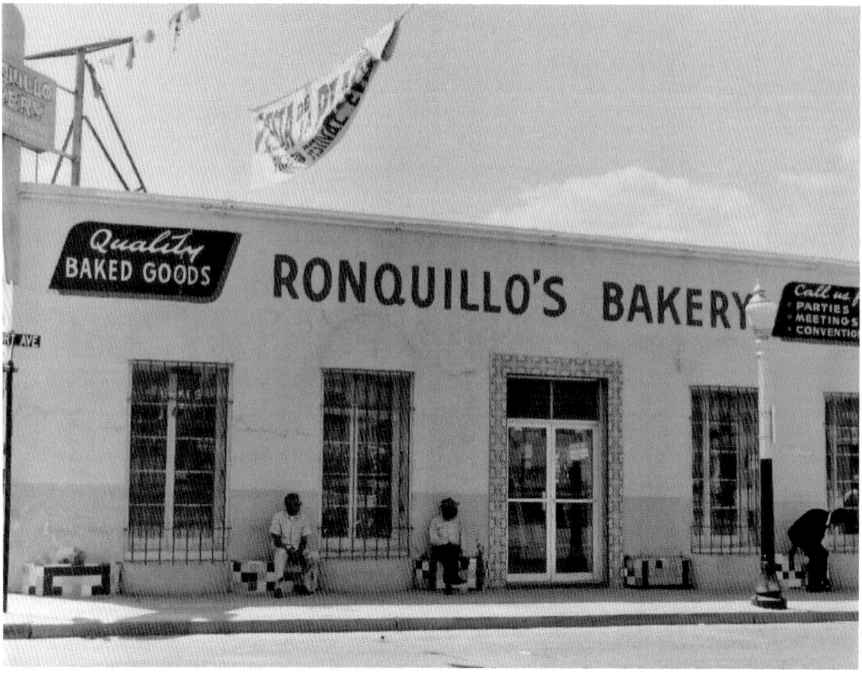

Mexican bakeries served as gathering spots for neighbors. *Walter L. Goodwin Jr., photographer, Ronquillo's Bakery, 1965. Commissioned by the Tucson Art Center. From the collection of the Tucson Museum of Art and Historic Block.*

Whiskey, Six-Guns and Red Light Ladies: George Hand's Saloon Diaries, 1875–1878 that the poor Mexicans did sell tamales and other food. And Hand mentions many dinners that consisted of enchiladas and tamales.[8]

Although Tucsonans were much more open-minded than folks just about anywhere else in the Southwest, for the poorer Mexicans life wasn't as easy. Classrooms weren't segregated as far as the Mexican and American populations, but speaking Spanish was strongly discouraged. Students may have noticed some preferential treatment toward whites.

In his paper "Barriers to Mexican Integration in Tucson," James Officer noted that although classrooms weren't segregated, kids tended to hang out with the kids who were like them. He noted also that the Mexican students who did have Anglo friends or who were standouts in school did so because they spoke English. With that in mind, he wrote, "I also believe teachers in elementary and high schools should insist that Mexican children speak English on the playground and in the classroom."[9] Whether that was enforced is uncertain.

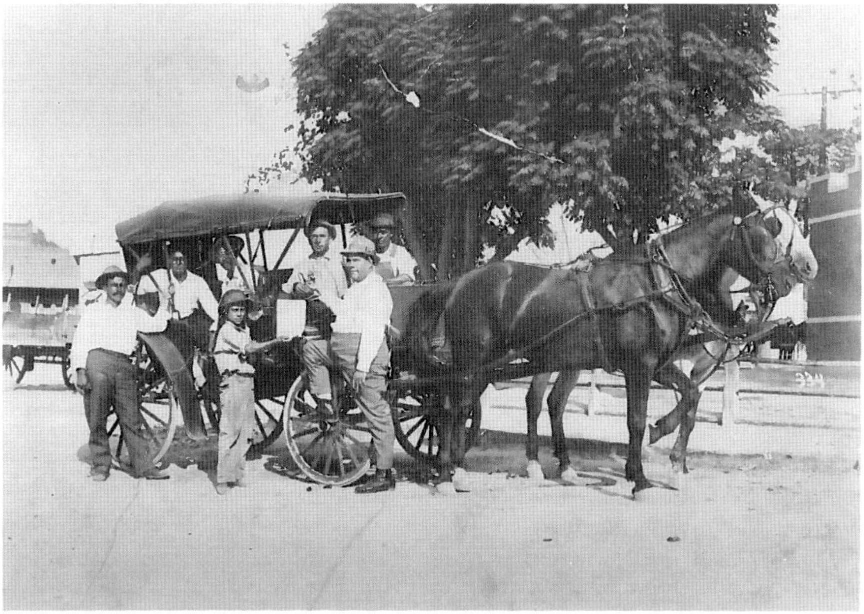

Romero's Taxi Service, 1910. *Photographer unknown. Gift of Mary Venuti, from the collection of the Tucson Museum of Art and Historic Block.*

A small African American population was also part of the mix. They worked mostly in service positions, but a few owned small businesses, including several restaurants. In the first part of his 1933 master's thesis "The Negro of Tucson, Past and Present," James Walter Yancy discussed the lives of African Americans in Tucson between the years 1850 and 1900. He estimated that by 1900 there were eighty-six "Negroes" (the common usage at the time) in Tucson. Most were male, many were former army veterans who served during the Civil War and several owned barbershops that exclusively served whites. He featured twenty of the more well-known African Americans, one of whom is known simply as Mrs. Lee.[10]

Mrs. Lee had come from Phoenix and, upon arrival, rented the dining room at the Orndorff Hotel. She did the cooking while employing "a number of colored waitresses. Over these waitresses she placed a Negro man." She developed a reputation of serving fine food and "received the patronage of the best people in Tucson."

But if African Americans weren't allowed equal access, the Chinese were outright reviled, especially in the territorial days. Letters in the *Arizona Citizen* were filled with hate and bigotry that don't bear quoting. Dates are a little

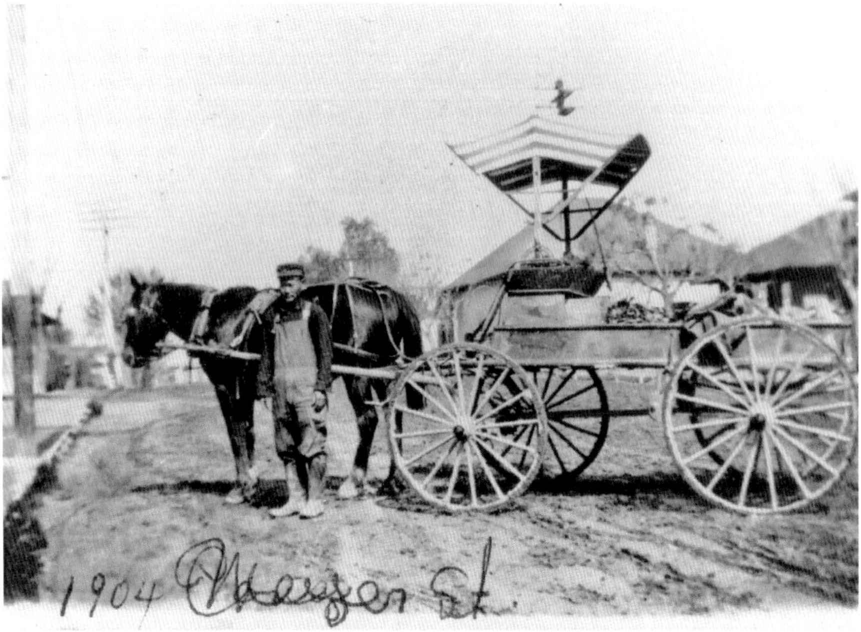

A Chinese truck farmer and his truck. *Arizona Historical Society.*

sketchy as to when the actual first Chinese arrived, but in the November 11, 1876 edition of the *Arizona Citizen*, there is an ad for the Celestial Restaurant run by Wong Tai. It was located on Congress Street near the Church Plaza, which was the heart of the city. Yet another ad from 1875 has the owner being Hop Kee & Company. By 1888, a restaurant called the OK Restaurant was at the same location.[11]

As the railroad was built through Arizona, Chinese workers left that hard, low-waged work and moved to Tucson for a chance at a better life. The numbers of Chinese in Tucson were small, plus they were thousands of miles away from their homeland. This necessitated creating bonds with the Mexican American community (in China, the concept is called *guanxi* and usually applies to other Chinese).

In addition to laundries, restaurants and other small businesses, the Chinese opened numerous neighborhood markets where Mexicans were regular customers. The two groups lived in a peaceful coexistence except when it came to the use of water (a most precious commodity in the desert). A number of Chinese also worked good-sized truck farms on leased land at the edge of the city. They grew a huge variety of fresh vegetables, which they sold to the general population, first door to door and then in the

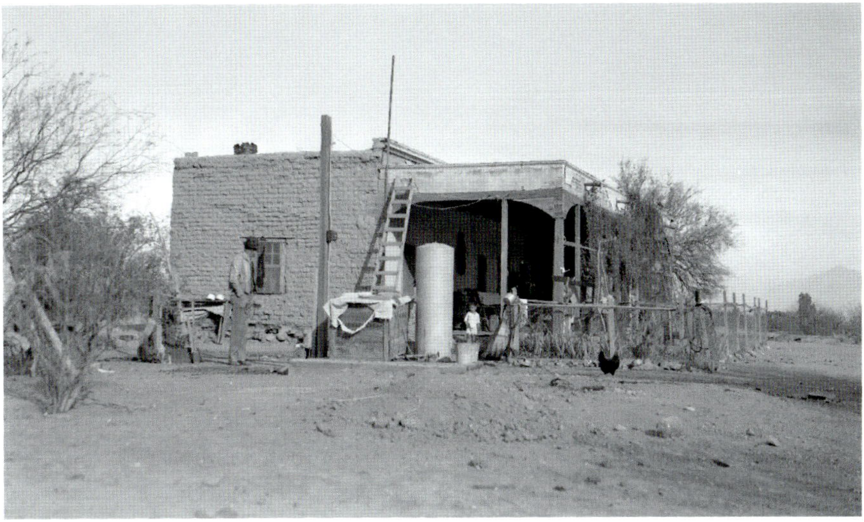

Leopoldo Carrillo's home. Carrillo leased his land to Chinese farmers for their truck farms. *Library of Congress.*

neighborhood markets. A sizable portion of land they used was leased from Leopoldo Carrillo.

Mexican farmers were angry at the amount of water the Chinese used. The fight went to court in *W.A. Dalton et al. v. Leopoldo Carrillo et al.* in 1885. Dalton's argument was that the Chinese used more than what they deserved—even stealing water if they needed it. Never mind that the produce the Chinese grew on Carrillo's land was more varied and that it was sold to the general public or that the water the Mexicans used was mainly for home gardens. There was a point to be made. Cooler heads prevailed, and the Chinese won.[12]

Other efforts to keep the Chinese in their place failed. In 1893, a petition was circulated to segregate all Chinese businesses to a specific area, but it was thrown out by the city council. On the national level, several exclusion acts limited the numbers of Chinese (and other "foreigners") from relocating to America and the kinds of jobs they could hold. A call also went out to secure the America-Mexico barrier to keep the Chinese from entering the United States via Mexico. A government patrol on horseback was created to catch anyone trying to sneak into the country. Still, people tried to enter by paying high fees to guides ("coyotes") to get them through the hostile desert. These actions mirror much of the same attitudes and actions that are prevalent today, although the guns

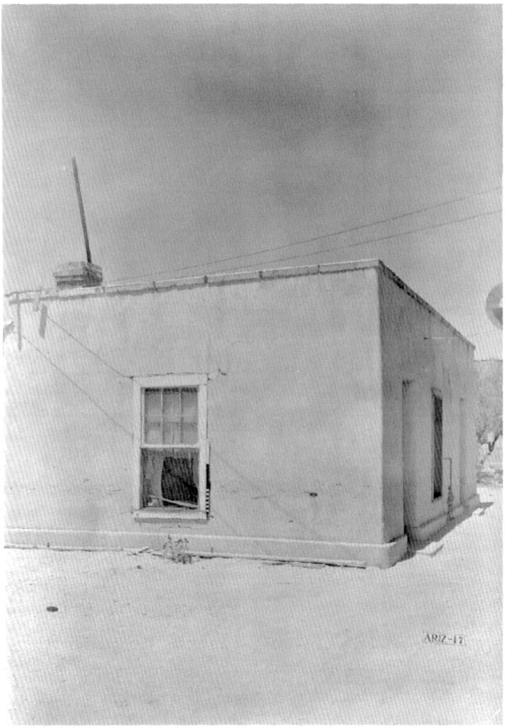

Left: Summer kitchen. *Library of Congress.*

Below: A historic house in Tucson all spiffed up. *Bill Lancaster, Creative Commons.*

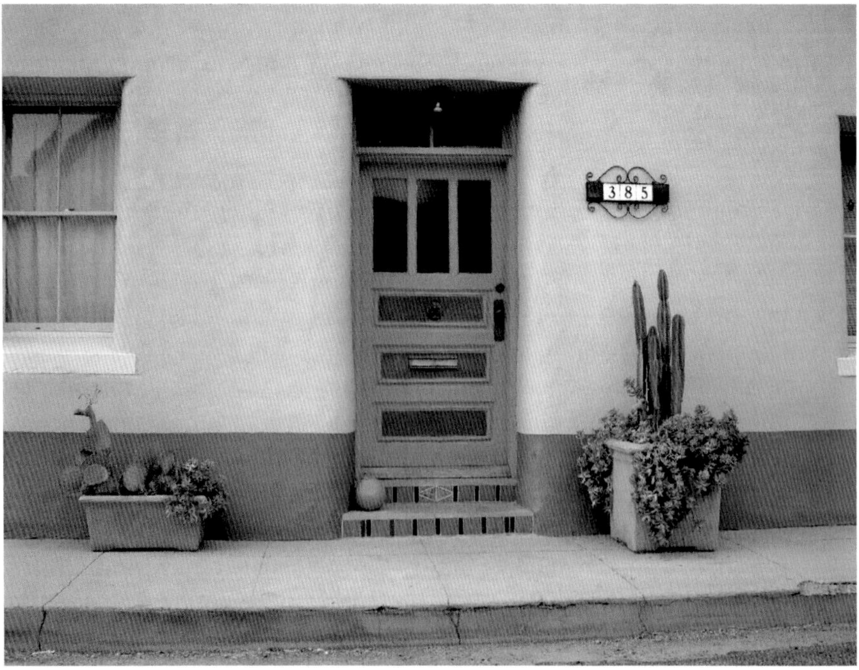

are bigger, drug smuggling is part of the movement and immigrants are Mexican (or from other parts of Central and South America).[13]

As one century ended and another began, things improved some, but life was still tough. Chinatown was located near the outskirts of downtown. The entire place was razed to build the Woman's Club, and the community moved elsewhere. But by 1927, two Chinese restaurants, the Peking and the Richilieu, were popular with a wide array of Tucsonans.[14]

Dining Halls, Restaurants and Saloons

Records of the first dining spots that weren't in boardinghouses and hotels are a little sketchy, but they show that a restaurant of some sort was torn down to make way for the Palace Hotel.

The Palace was the first hotel built for the purpose of being a hotel locally. Until then, accommodations had been rooms in peoples' homes, reconverted buildings, stables and the street, depending on how much money one had. Meals were included.[15]

The restaurant at the Palace had ninety seats and a "substantial menu." In an advertisement in the April 10, 1880 edition of the *Arizona Citizen*, the call-out reads, "The spacious dining hall is under supervision of an accomplished steward, the cuisine is excellent and the waiters are attentive and polite." Who could ask for more?

About that same time, another restaurant of note, and perhaps the only rival to the elegant dining room at the Palace, was attracting diners. It was called the Shoo Fly because of the many flies that were also attracted to the place. In a column in the September 21, 1958 edition of the *Arizona Daily Star*, Audrey Hunter described the Shoo Fly as rustic. She noted, "The tables were covered with cheap but clean cloths in the morning, but by evening were grey with dust that was thicker than the flies." The menu consisted of an assortment of canned seafood including sardines, oysters and lobster. Mexican-style beans were also served; fresh vegetables and fruit were dear.[16]

A restaurant could also be found at Levin's Garden. Opened in 1866 by Alex Levin, the park was located in the west side of the city, a site now occupied by government buildings, apartment houses and historic homes.[17] Levin was a Prussian immigrant who had come to Tucson via Mexico. The grounds were beautiful thanks to trees planted by Levin. Citizens could enjoy a bowling alley, an archery range, a shooting range and a saloon, complete

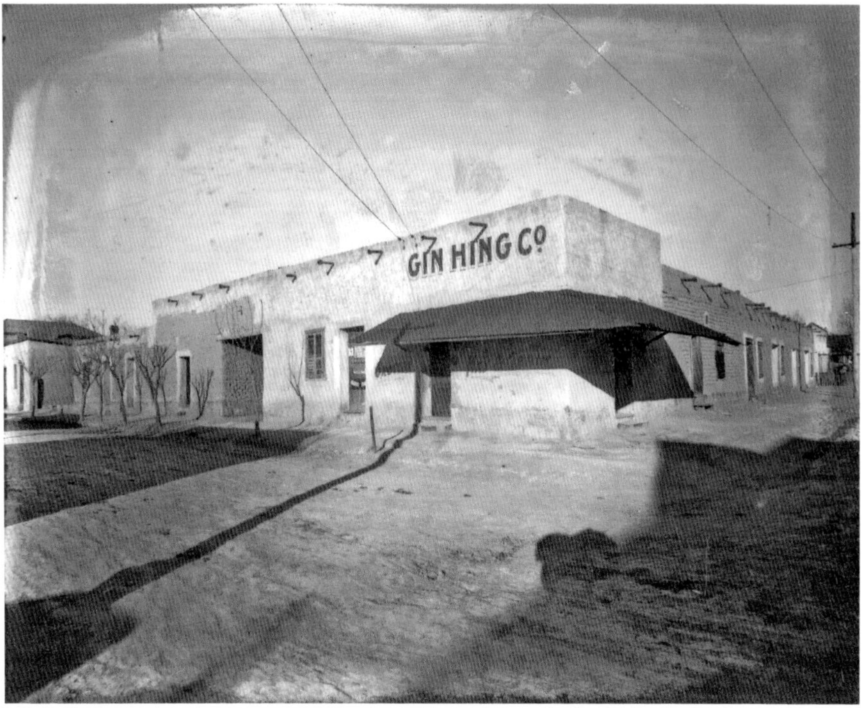

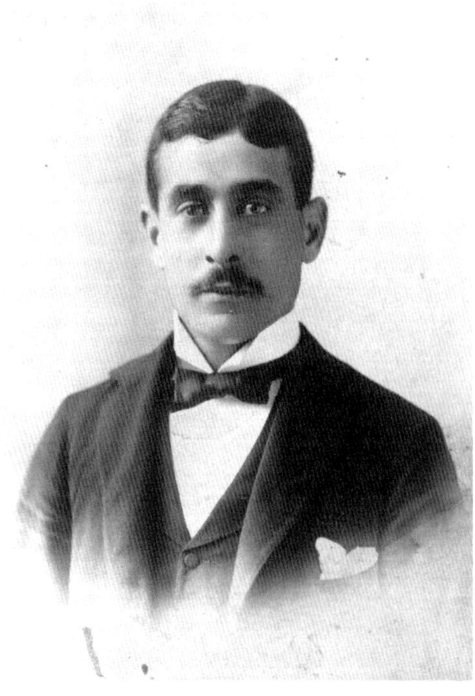

Above: Street scene in downtown Tucson, circa 1878. *Arizona Historical Society*.

Left: Alex Levin, one of the early pioneers of Tucson. His Levin's Garden was the entertainment center of its time. *Arizona Historical Society*.

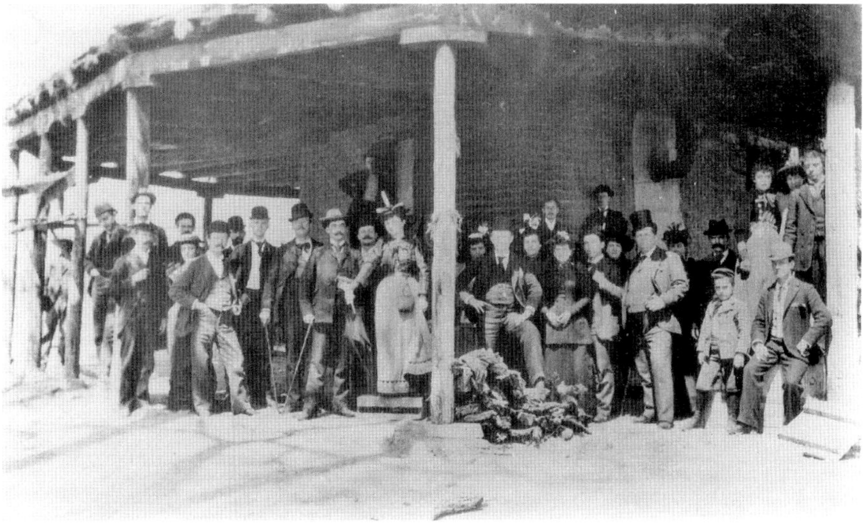

A night at Levin's Garden. *Arizona Historical Society.*

with a brothel and a restaurant. Not much is known about the restaurant, but Levin's wife, who was from Mexico, ran the place and served food that paired well with poker playing and beer drinking. Levin had a very successful brewery as well. Over the years, he also operated several saloons. His beer was said to be some of the best in town.[18]

Hospitality must run in the blood because Levin's descendants ran restaurants well into the 2000s. His daughter, Sophia, got the first liquor license in the state after Prohibition. (Details of the family restaurants can be found in next chapter.)

George Hand, one of the many saloonkeepers in town—and there were plenty of saloons—kept a diary that was later transcribed by Neal Carmody in the book *Whiskey, Six-Guns and Red Light Ladies*. He described many meals he enjoyed between getting drunk, breaking up fights and waiting for mail to arrive via stagecoach. While he seldom notes where he ate, Hand spent many hours at Joseph Neugass's Tucson Restaurant. Neugass, who later became a territorial judge and had dealings with the Earp family in Tombstone, eventually moved his restaurant to "the new hotel." Historians think that meant the Palace.[19]

Hand also talks about eating at the Kaiser Wilhelm, which in 1878 was owned by Otto Von Reichenbach. On one evening in July 1876, Hand notes that he "ate dinner at the Chinaman's" and called it "a good meal." Carmody suggested that the restaurant was probably the Celestial.[20] Saloons also often served some types of foods, although no record shows what was served. Either way, the diaries give us some great insight into the culinary offerings in the Old Pueblo before statehood.

Competition was stiff for diners, and restaurants began to advertise. In the April 4, 1879 edition of the *Arizona Citizen*, ads could be found for the Exchange Restaurant on Congress and Meyer, the New California Restaurant ("formerly Barnum's") and Nellie Cashman's the Delmonico, where "the best meals in the city can be obtained.... The tables are supplied with everything the market offers.[21]

By 1880, both the Gem Saloon and the Pima Bank Exchange were serving German meals.[22]

Coming of Age

Tucson was the territorial capital from 1867 to 1877. Then, through some political finagling, the powers that be had the capital moved to Prescott. Of course, this didn't sit well with people in Tucson, and they demanded another vote. The trouble was that the representatives who were sent to Prescott never made it due to a huge snowstorm and other glitches. Tucson lost the capital.

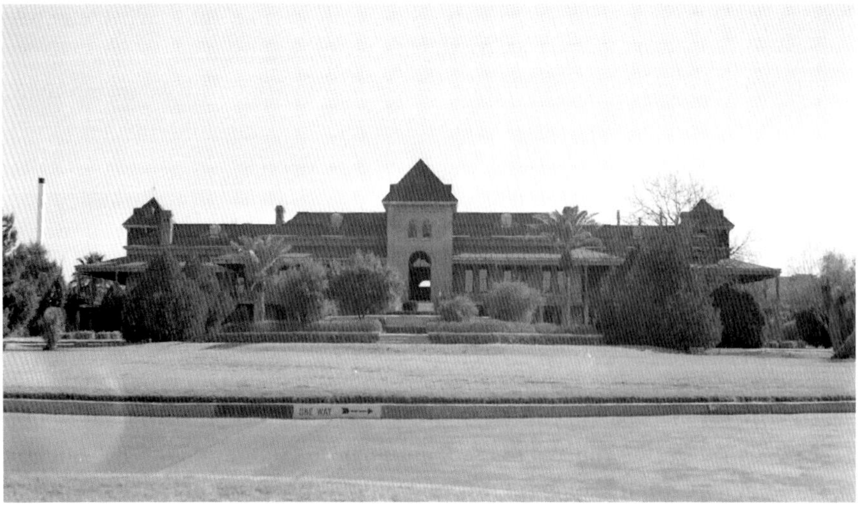

Old Main on the University of Arizona Campus, circa 1940. When the university opened in 1891, Old Main was the only building. *Library of Congress.*

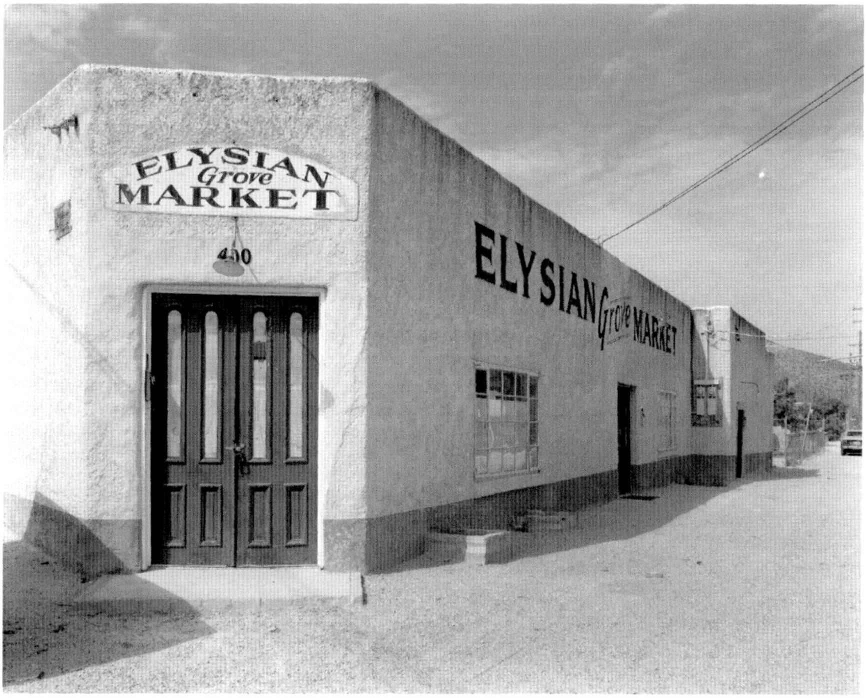

Elysian Grove Market. *Library of Congress.*

As a token gesture, the legislature granted Tucson the university. People weren't pleased, but they bit the proverbial bullet. In 1891, the University of Arizona opened some four miles from the center of the city.[23] In the long run, Tucson got the better deal, as the university widened Tucson's horizons. Students and faculty from all over the world brought their cultures to the Old Pueblo, which included food.

The Railroad Arrives and Nothing Is Ever the Same

On March 20, 1880, with much pomp and circumstance, the Southern Pacific Railroad chugged into town.[24] With it came fancier folks, better building materials, Milwaukee beer and ice. Tucson went from being a low-slung adobe village to a more refined "city," complete with all the trimmings.

Prior to the railroad, and due to a number of German residents, Tucson was home to numerous breweries. Once the trains arrived with goods from

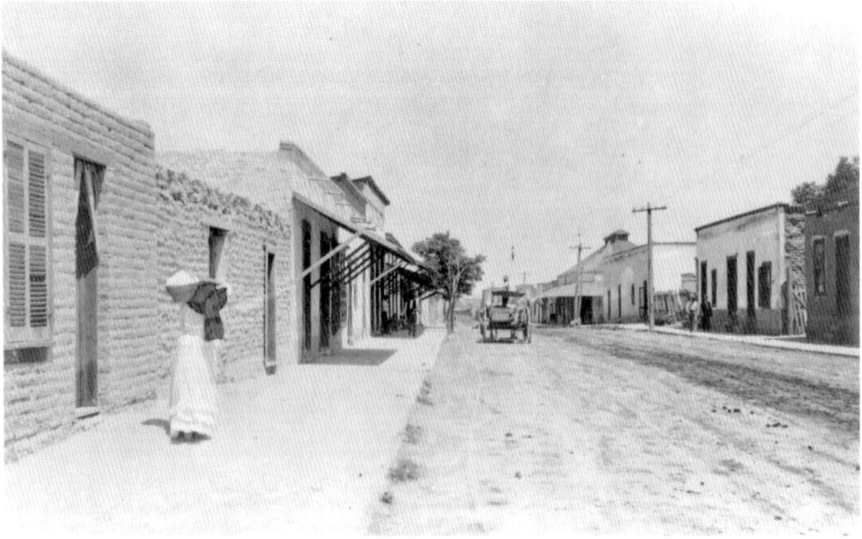

Meyer Street. *Library of Congress.*

back east—and with them the ability to keep things cold and fresh—beer was "imported" from Milwaukee. Many breweries went out of business. But for the most part, it was the railroad that changed Tucson. An 1881 city directory called Tucson "the only city of importance between Los Angeles in California and San Antonio in Texas."[25]

During this time (the early 1880s through the first part of the 1900s), other modern comforts such as the telephone, electric lights and running water arrived. A Carnegie Library had been built. There were two daily newspapers and even sidewalks. *Out West* magazine called Tucson "one of the most modern, progressive, prosperous and law-abiding cities to be found in the length and breadth of the land."[26]

On February 14, 1912, Arizona became the forty-eighth state. Tucson was ready for the twentieth century.

Modern Times: 1920s–1950s

The Tucson City Directory reported that in 1924 there were thirty-five restaurants.[27] Most were downtown, but the college crowd had a few favorites near campus: the Copper Kettle, the Varsity Inn and the Yucca Tea Room.

The Varsity helped put a lot of people through college. It lasted through the late 1960s but had by that time become a "greasy spoon" according to Dr. Jim Griffith, a former University of Arizona professor and Tucson's most famous folklorist. He recalled eating many a bologna sandwich there.[28]

Yancy, in the second part of his thesis that covers African Americans in the 1930s, discussed "Negro businesses," three of which were restaurants. He simply labeled them Restaurants A, B and C. Restaurant A was located on Convent Street, which is slightly west of the downtown area. The interior of the restaurant is described as "not so appealing to anyone seeking food." The space was small, the floors were "filthy, and there are grease spots all over them." The rest of the space didn't fare much better in terms of cleanliness, but the location was "desirable being near the places which Negroes frequent the most." There were two employees. Yancy also discussed the profit margin, which was slim; the number of meals served on an average day; and the patronage, which according to him was "95% colored, and 5% Mexican."

In Yancy's opinion, Restaurant B fared a little better on all counts. Also located on Convent Street, it had a "barby-cue" pit in the front dining area. The space was even tinier than Restaurant A's, but it was a little cleaner; the only employee was the owner. Meals were comparable in price to Restaurant A.

And then there is Restaurant C. Located on Sabino Street, which is now where the Tucson Convention Center is located, this restaurant was run by "a Negro woman who has eight years of this kind of experience." Yancy found this restaurant to be practically perfect in terms of cleanliness, space and income versus costs. Plus there was music. Restaurant C was the only one that Yancy thought had any chance of succeeding for a length of time.[29] There is some evidence that two were named Peggy Watson's Chat & Chew Café and Jimmy's Chicken Shack.[30] Jim Crow was also evident. Theaters were segregated. Kids were only allowed to use public pools on the day before the pools were drained.

In 1950, "You couldn't get buy a cup of coffee," said Charles Kendrick, co-founder of the Heritage Museum and lifelong resident of Tucson. Kendrick recalled that even the University of Arizona, where he matriculated in 1950, wouldn't serve African Americans and that the only place where African Americans were able to enjoy a meal out was Duke Shaw's. In about 1952 or so, Kendrick heard from a friend that a woman, whose name he couldn't recall, had two restaurants (one called Spanish Trail and the other one was downtown) that would serve African Americans. Frampton-Stone Cafeteria followed shortly.[31] This separation continued until well into the 1960s. In 1963, the National Association for the Advancement of Colored People (NAACP) and locals demonstrated outside the Pickwick Inn, located on the Southside. The day after the restaurant changed its policy, the city council passed an ordinance outlawing the practice of not serving people because of their race or ethnicity.[32]

The first half of the twentieth century was an exciting time for Tucsonans. In 1919, the first municipal airport in the country was established. In 1927, Davis-Monthan Air Force base began operations. Like the university, DM, as locals call it, added residents and world influences to the mix. In 1934, John Dillinger was captured when a fire started at the Hotel Congress where he and his gang were hiding out. Then, in 1939, Columbia Pictures built a movie set west of the Tucson Mountains for the movie *Arizona*. That film was the first of many that were shot in and around Tucson. Old Tucson became the site of many movies and a major tourist attraction. Movie stars had to eat somewhere, and there are plenty of stories about everyone from John Wayne to Paul Newman dining all over town.

Two restaurants even had "roles" in movies. In 1956, a scene from *A Kiss Before Dying* was filmed at the Pago Pago. And in *Alice Doesn't Live Here Anymore*, Alice worked at Mel's Diner, which was really Big Al's BBQ on Main Street. That film was director Martin Scorsese's first movie. Many more films followed, as did television shows, such as *The High Chaparral*, *Little House on the Prairie* and *Petrocelli*.

Tourists came in droves, thanks to the Tucson Sunshine Climate Club, a group of local businessmen who contributed $1,000 to the organization with the sole purpose of attracting visitors. And it worked. Motels and restaurants seemed to pop up everywhere. One of the more popular areas, a section where U.S. Highways 80 and 89 and Arizona Highway 84 merged, was dubbed Miracle Mile. Several restaurants featured in this book were located along this stretch of roadside of Americana.[33] In 1947, professional baseball came to Tucson in the form of spring training, adding hundreds of thousands of dollars to the hospitality industry. It continued until 2010.

In 1950, the population of Tucson was 45,454; by 1960, it had exploded to 212,892. Remarkable indeed. In many ways, that decade was the beginning of the modern restaurant era.[34]

More Mouths to Feed

The 1960s saw major changes in Tucson. In 1961, Interstate 10 was completed. It changed surface street traffic immediately, which affected many small businesses. In 1960, El Con Mall was built on the site of the once elegant El Conquistador hotel on Broadway, forever changing Tucsonan's shopping habits. In 1970, Speedway Boulevard was named the "Ugliest Street in America" by *Life* magazine. Tucson was also one of a handful of cities that was awarded a Model Cities grant. While the grant modernized parts of the core of Tucson, it never fulfilled the goals that had been laid out due to a change of administrations—from Johnson to Nixon—and mismanagement.

From an interview with Richard Fe Tom, July 2015.

The intent of the urban renewal of the late 1960s was to improve the city and the lives of its citizens. But in the rush to make peoples' lives better, much history was lost. Congress Street, west of Stone Avenue, held many small businesses that became the victims of these "improvements."

The Plaza Theater, the only theater in southern Arizona that exclusively showed Spanish-language movies, was torn down in May 1969, according to the March 1, 1969 *Arizona Daily Star*. Two doors down was the Old Peking restaurant, which had been in business (at another location) since 1927. In 1960, the original owner, John Shue, sold the Old Peking to Raymond N. Tom. Tom, who had been born in China, worked in various industries in the San Francisco area. This included his time in the army during World War II, where he was a welder in the shipyards. His son, Richard Fe Tom, isn't sure when his father arrived in Tucson, but he remembered the family grocery store on the Southside and then his dad buying the Old Peking around 1960.

A sign out front advertised chop suey and noodles, but the menu included many American favorites. All meals, including the popular wieners and rice, came with mashed potatoes, a bowl of soup, two sides and bread and butter. This dish was exactly what it said it was; gravy was included. It cost a whopping fifty-five cents.

The fried chicken was also popular. Tom recalled the chicken being quartered and then served one quarter to a person. He spent many hours working there after school. He said the restaurant opened at 6:00 a.m. and closed at 9:00 p.m. His father was there all day, from a few hours before opening to well after closing. Fe said that his dad loved the work and working with the customers, some of whom became friends. But the Peking was on "the list," and although Fe doesn't remember when it was torn down, the proximity to the Plaza suggests that it was probably around the same time.

The Toms didn't own the building, so they didn't receive compensation. Fe regretted that they left everything behind, including a vintage jukebox and the cash register. Raymond went on to open another grocery store in Silverbell, Arizona, a mining town more than twenty-five miles away. He drove there and back to Tucson every day. Silverbell is now a ghost town. Today, government buildings sit near where the Old Peking operated. A sign of urban renewal, perhaps, but also a sad monument to a truly lost restaurant.

Tucson also experienced a boom in fine dining options during this time. Even though some of the edge-of-town roads where the restaurants were located were still dirt, Tucsonans dined in high style. People expected more than just a good meal. They also wanted to be entertained. Live music was almost required if restaurateurs wanted to fill their dining rooms. Dancing was a big part of the experience, and themed restaurants also popped up. Steakhouse drew tourists and locals alike. Ethnic restaurants were pretty much limited to Mexican, Chinese and Italian.

Miracle Mile

This strip of road was once a thriving corridor of hospitality. Small motor courts in the 1930s and 1940s gave way to some of the city's most popular restaurants from the late 1950s through the 2000s. Detailed accounts of the restaurants will follow, but today, with the exception of a longtime Mexican restaurant, Club 21, none of the hot spots exists.

Restaurant Row

By the mid-1970s, the Eastside of Tucson was booming. Tanque Verde Road, which starts where Wilmot Road meets Pima Street, soon became known as Restaurant Row as dozens of hip, modern places opened. Bobby McGee's, Jester's Court, the Solarium, the Pawnbroker, the Cork 'n Cleaver, Tail of the Cock, the Nantucket Lobster Trap (later Jerome's and then Fuego) and Dakota joined more established places like Sneaky Pete's, Pinnacle Peak's, the Monaco Inn and The Tack Room, creating a dining and dancing mecca. Of that long list, only Dakota and Pinnacle Peak remain.[35]

1980s and Beyond

Tucson restaurants were affected deeply by the recession of the late '70s and early '80s. Restaurants tried to hang on; some lasted, others shuttered. Tastes changed, and more chains popped up all over town. Local restaurants were beginning to feel the pinch.

Then, in 1996, after reading an article in *Tucson Monthly*, Councilman Steve Leal became concerned and called a meeting of the powers that be—that is, owners and chefs from local independent restaurants. At that meeting were Deb Gellman of Presidio Grill, Alan Zeman of Fuego, John Jacob of El Parador and Don Luria of Café Terra Cotta. The executive director of Arizona Restaurant Association–Southern Division, Rob LeMaster; John Hudak of Madden Publishing; and the article's author, Mike Munday, were also at the table. Nothing was settled at that first meeting except the common goal of "preserving the flavors of Tucson." Hudak made a grand gesture and for one year ran two full-page four-color ads for the restaurants, gratis. This was the shot in the arm that the group needed.

Luria gathered together thirty-five independent restaurants and set up a press conference announcing the organization of the Tucson Originals.[36] Gone was the concept of competitions among local independent restaurants. The purpose of this unique group was to promote Tucson and to create advantages for independents that only chains have—for example, buying quantities of food as a group to get better prices.

The other goal, and perhaps the most important, was to highlight the unique tastes that Tucson had to offer. That was like asking Picasso to paint a masterpiece because the chefs involved were already doing that on a daily basis. The Originals also banged its own drum by making diners aware of the financial impact local restaurants make. Finally, the chefs wanted to teach kids all about "eating local."

They elected the perfect person as president: Don Luria. Don added not just creativity and love of good food but also a deep business sense. A few rules were established: one, serving on a committee; two, participation in a group event; and three, writing a check to the community food bank. The fifty dollars were well worth it.

The group met with such great success that soon Luria was traveling all over the United States helping restaurants in other cities do the same. Luria is no longer involved with the group, but the Originals keeps on in a somewhat less powerful form. And while many of the original Originals' sites have closed (including Luria's iconic Terra Cotta) or moved on, the group has kept many restaurants in business, some to this very day.

Chapter 2

Mexican Restaurants

Do You Like Chimichangas?

Before this chapter begins, one thing must be established: Tucson Mexican food is *not* Tex-Mex, nor is it Cal-Mex or New Mexican–Mex. If you are smart, you won't use any of those terms around locals. Tucson Mexican fare comes from Sonora, Mexico, the state directly across the border. While it may be hard to define what the differences are, typically the tortillas are flour; the meat is beef; corn, when it is used, is yellow; and although chiles are used with everything, they are mild and come both dried and fresh.

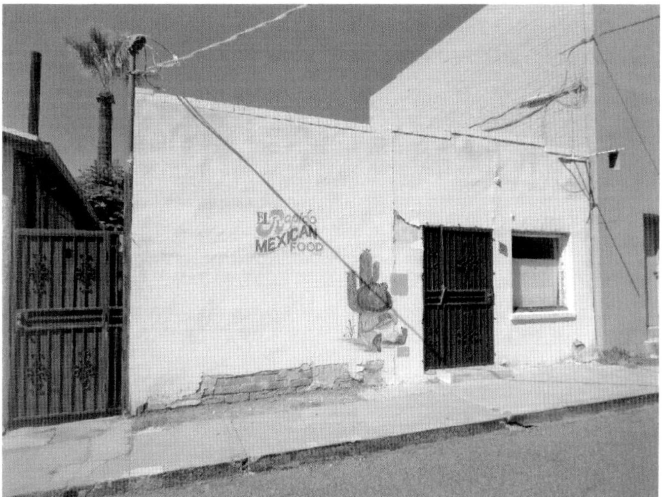

El Rapido, where those in the know went for fresh tortillas. *Paul Sableman, Creative Commons.*

In *Whiskey, Six-Guns and Red Light Ladies*, Hand writes about daily meals; dinner often consists of enchiladas and beans. Neal Carmody, who transcribed the book, noted that Mexican women sold tamales and other Mexican fare, most likely from their homes or door to door. The restaurant at Levin's Garden also served Mexican dishes, as Levin's wife, who ran the restaurant, was from Mexico.[37]

Bryan Mezon, Alex Levin's great-great-grandson, said that the first Mexican restaurant in Tucson was run by Levin's daughter, Sophia. It was called La Conquista, although records show that there may have been others prior to La Conquista.[38]

Remarkably, many of the Mexican restaurants that started in the 1920s and 1930s are still in operation. Grandchildren and great-grandchildren serve the same dishes their grandparents served. Many of these restaurants are located in South Tucson, the square-mile city within a city. It's a tribute to traditions and family love that keep these places around. Of course, not all restaurants survived. But memories have.

1920s–1930s

La Cazuela Tea Room

This tiny spot was opened on a whim in 1926. Miss Yndia Smalley wanted to open a restaurant, even though she knew nothing about the business—or even how to cook, for that matter. But the idea of having a tearoom appealed to her. So, in March 1926, Smalley and her friend Malcolm Cummings opened La Cazuela on South Sixth Street just outside downtown. Smalley was a daughter of one of the city's prominent families, and Cummings's father was the president of the University of Arizona.[39]

Smalley hired a woman from Mexico to do all the cooking. The place quickly outgrew itself, and the restaurant was moved to a historic home on Main Street. Smalley claimed that a patio wall was part of the original presidio that housed troops. Smalley also claimed that her cook invented almendrado, the fluffy, gelatin-like dessert that has the colors of the Mexican flag topped with a sweet almond sauce.[40]

The restaurant was moved to a historic house, the Fish House, when business got too big for the original room. The floors were sawdust, the walls were rough adobe and a statue of Saint Anthony stood in the entry, as was

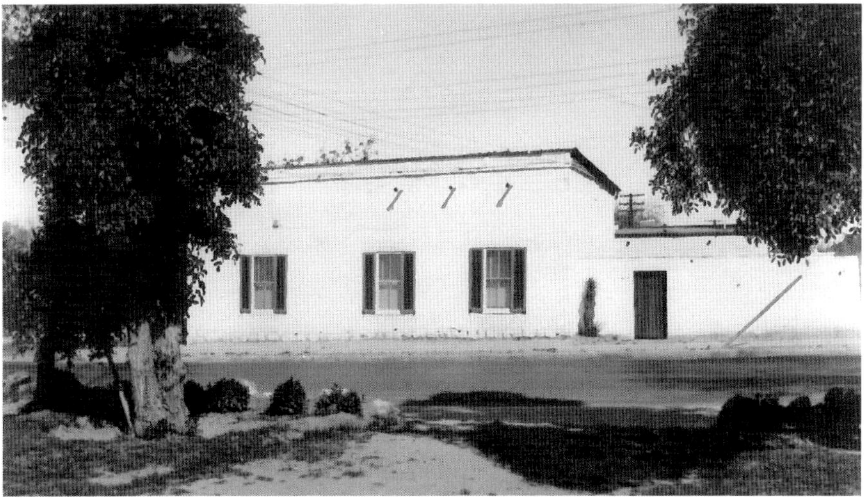

Above: Years before this photo was taken, the Fish House was home to La Cazuela Tea Room for one season. Donated by Ysidero Romero, 1935. *From the collection of the Tucson Museum of Art and Historic Block.*

Right: Sophia Levin, daughter of Alex Levin. Her restaurant, La Conquista, got the first liquor license in the state of Arizona after the Volstead Act was repealed. *Arizona Historical Society.*

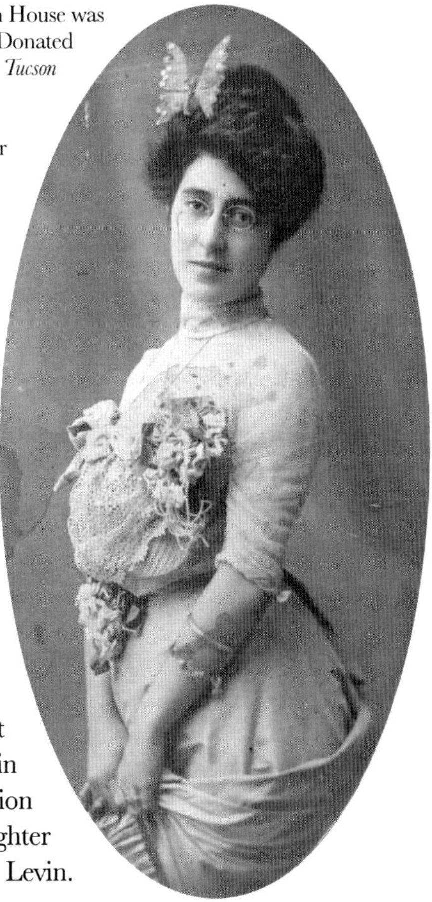

the custom of Mexican businesses. Smalley wanted to keep the feel of a "humble Mexican home." She abandoned her tearoom when her father decided that it was costing him too much money.[11]

La Conquista

Sophia Pérez's restaurant was the first establishment to get a liquor license in the state of Arizona once Prohibition was repealed.[12] Pérez was the daughter of Tucson's king of hospitality, Alex Levin.

Her mother, Zenona Molina, was also from a famous restaurant family in Tucson. And she was the mother of René Pérez, who owned and operated Papagayo restaurant. In fact, the recipes used at Papagayo were Sophia's recipes.

1940s

Pancho's

In 1947, most Mexican restaurants in Tucson were in or around South Tucson. But after having met with some success with two restaurants downtown, Frank "Pancho" Gonzales, along with his wife, Julietta, opened a small Mexican restaurant on Grant Road.

Measuring only forty by fifty feet, Pancho's served traditional Sonoran fare. Pancho and Julietta were the only employees. They cooked, cleaned and waited on tables (tables that they had made themselves, mind you). Long hours and hard work were a regular part of the day.[13] But Frank was no stranger to hard work. He'd been working since he was seven. He was born in Mexico while his widowed mother was on her way to Tucson. The small family lived a hard life with barely a roof over their heads. Frank, at the age of seven, started shining shoes, and the rest is history. He did everything from washing school buses to caddying golf, eventually getting a job with the city parks system. The contacts he made there would last him the rest of his life.

And then he and Julietta decided to open Pancho's.[14] They must've been quite successful, as they had six employees by the end of the first year. Frank noted in a 1969 article in the *Tucson Citizen* that some of those same employees were still there. Years passed. Two sons (Frank and Ronald) were born. And the business got bigger.

People from all over the city were drawn to Pancho's, not just because of the great food but because of Frank's affable personality. He knew everyone and treated his guests like friends. Dining at Pancho's was a good time; everyone had fun whether you were a guest or an employee.[15]

The menus at one time were made of fans. Another had a smiling Mexican man in a big sombrero. Pancho's became known for its barbacoa. Specialty items included Enchiladas Montadas, three flat enchiladas topped with a fried egg, the house enchilada sauce and sour cream. The topopo, a tower

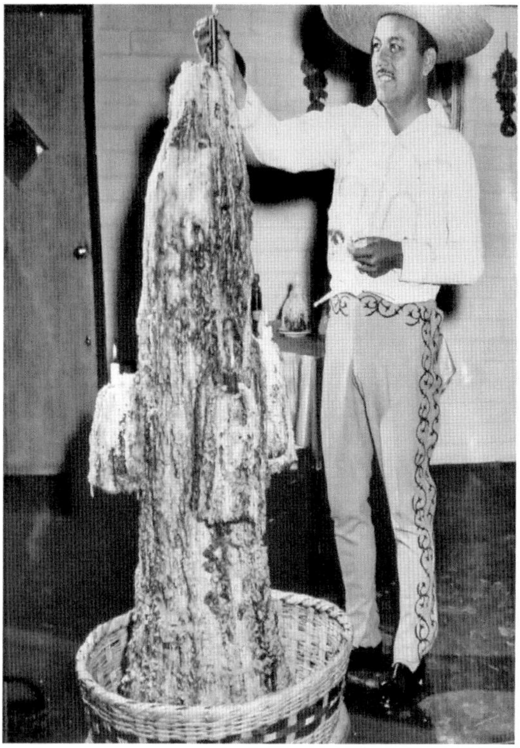

Pancho lights the World's Largest Dripping Candle. *Marco Bravo, photographer. The Gonzales family.*

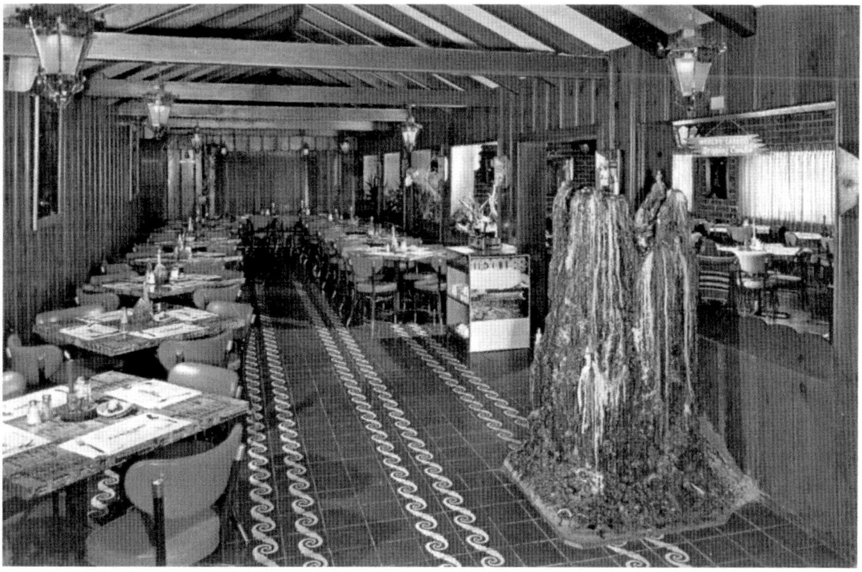

Pancho's dining room and the World's Largest Dripping Candle. *From the collection of Dwight and Christy Schannep, Arizona Antique Mall.*

of salad that sat on a bean tostada, had lettuce, chicken, cheese, avocados, jalapeños and the special house dressing. If you wanted it topped with chile con carne, it would cost you thirty cents more (in 1990 at least).[16]

Somewhere along the line, no one is quite sure when, Frank Sr. began what came to be known as the symbol for Pancho's: the famous dripping candle. It grew to be nearly as tall as Frank and was dubbed the tallest dripping candle in existence.

Pancho was active in the community and even served on the city council, holding the seat of vice-mayor for a short while. Not bad for a kid who started out shining shoes. The business eventually grew into three restaurants. One was on Broadway Boulevard, a second was on Twenty-second Street at Alvernon and a new building was up the street from the original site. This third Pancho's was much bigger than that first little restaurant. The tables were copper-topped. The artwork included pieces by Rivera (not Diego) and old velvet paintings of bullfighters—very traditional yet totally modern.

Frank's son, also called Frank, managed the restaurant on Broadway. He then got his kids into the act. The third Frank (Pancho's grandson) remembered cutting corn for the corn tamales when he was barely five. As soon as he was tall enough, they let him bus tables for a whopping twenty-five cents per table. He eventually became a manager.

Then, in April 1969, Frank Sr. died. The community lost a great man, and the family lost a figurehead. But they kept going as a tribute to the man who made Pancho's so successful.[17] Sometime in the '70s—Frank III wasn't sure exactly when—they built the Uno Mas Lounge. On one side, there was a stage perfect for live music. It was a very happening scene.

Like his father, Frank Jr. was well-loved and highly respected, and he believed in giving back to the city that had given him so much. His work with the Tucson Conquistadors, a huge service organization, is legendary. The group sponsored a yearly golf tournament, the Tucson Open, with a celebrity host. In the years Frank was a part of the event, Dean Martin was host. Martin frequented Pancho's, often bringing his Rat Pack friends with him. Is that Frank Sinatra over there with Sammy Davis Jr.?

Pancho's continued to bring in the crowds and was a repeat winner in the Taco Olympics, sponsored by the local newspaper. By the time Frank sold the business, the two Eastside restaurants had closed and another one on Oracle Road had opened. The new owners named the place Las Margaritas, but for many Tucsonans, it remains "the place that used to be Pancho's."

Frank Jr. died in 2010. Frank III now continues the family tradition with a restaurant in Charleston, West Virginia, called Mi Cocina de Amor (My

Kitchen of Love).[48] He uses the same recipes his grandfather used. "Grandma Julietta's Enchiladas" are on the menu. It may be in a different city and with a different name, but Pancho's lives on.

1950s–1960s

Araneta's Mexico Inn

From an interview with Michelle Araneta and Ginger and Michael Master, July 2015.

Long before vegetarianism became a lifestyle, well before Paula Deen added "love" as a main ingredient and decades before an open kitchen was all part of restaurant design, Alfonso and Rachelle Araneta were making refried beans without lard and using love not just as a main ingredient but as the tag line on their business cards; diners could also watch their enchiladas being built and melted to perfection because the main kitchen was out in the open.

The Aranetas opened their doors in 1955. In the early years, they were open twenty-four hours a day, and there were carhops. But by time I worked there in the 1970s, there was no evidence of either. The only problem for the drive-in customers was that if you were parked in the first row, you had to hope that those behind you allowed for a space to drive out.[49]

Alfonso inspected each bean by hand. A dried red chile was quickly sautéed in vegetable oil to add that secret something. The guacamole was made fresh every day. Al used a river rock to crush garlic that he used in his dishes. Tortillas, both flour and whole wheat, were piled high. The green onions for the salsa were cut to the precise standards set by Rachelle. It was hard work, but the results were well worth it.

Located just up the street from the University of Arizona, the Mexico Inn attracted students and faculty alike. There was definitely a diner look to the place, with its coral-toned vinyl booths and a counter that no one ever seemed to use. Huge windows wrapped around two sides of the building, allowing for views of the traffic on Speedway. A jukebox stood against one wall. A huge "painting" of the famous bullfighter Manuelito hung above it.

Specialties included dishes named for their daughters—Roanna, Ginger and Michelle—as well as staff members and special customers. The Mexico Inn was also famous for its enchilada sauce and, in season, green corn tamales. Michelle Araneta remembered going with her dad to buy the fresh

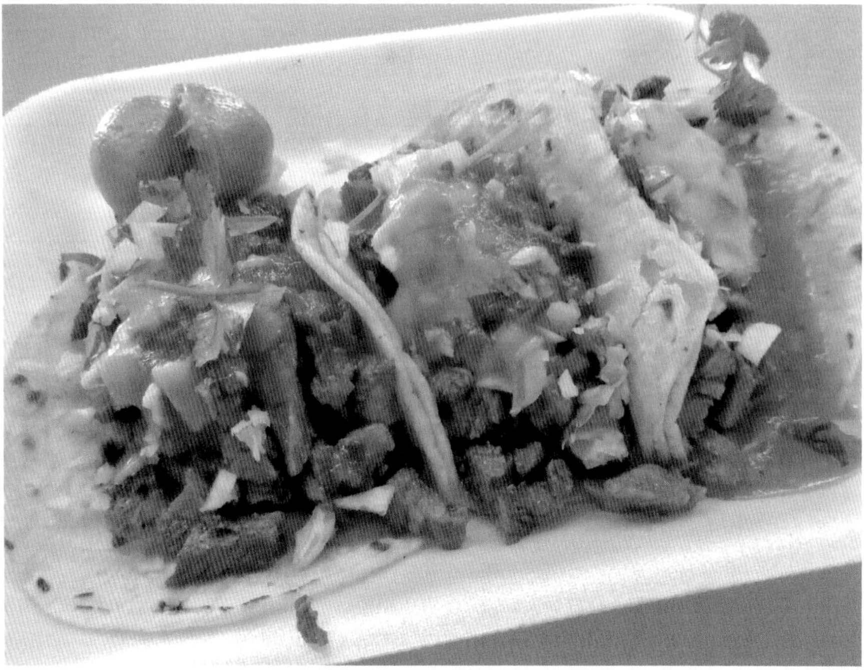

Tacos. *Author's collection.*

green corn. They'd fill the trunk with burlap sacks of corn and return to the shop, where her job was to clean away the husks and the silk. She tried to keep the little corn worms that she found as pets.[50] By the early 1970s, hours had been reduced to lunch and dinner, Tuesdays through Saturdays, with a break in between.

Al was always there with a story, usually with a moral or at least something to educate the listeners. One, which he told to the local newspaper, concerned how a shabby young man came in one evening and said that he had a busload of people but no money; he was hoping they could give them all some food. Things were tight at the time for the Aranetas, but they agreed. The young man left, but then he basically disappeared. Right after that, business got really busy. His daughters corroborated the story.[51]

Another story that daughters Michelle and Ginger Master told was of two women who arrived one evening. They were dressed in black and told the Aranetas that if they wanted to succeed in business, certain "rules" had to be followed. One was to never sweep the restaurant at night or else the profits would go out the door. They never swept at night after that. Michelle also noted that from that day forward, there wasn't a day that went by that

Al didn't give at least one meal free to someone.[52] No famous customers ever came in, but there were many intriguing regulars.

Time passed, and a second generation of young girls, the granddaughters, could be found every day "helping" in the kitchen. Alfonso taught cooking classes for many years at Pima Community College, where he shared some—but not all—of his secrets. Both Aranetas were active in various charitable organizations throughout the city.

By the time they retired in 1992, the restaurant was only open for dinner four days a week. Alfonso also spent his life writing a cookbook. Son-in-law Michael Master said that in 1993, Alfonso and Rachelle were planning on visiting them back east, where Alfonso planned on finishing the book. But shortly before they were to leave, Alfonso died. He was one month short of turning seventy-five years old.[53] Rachelle died about five years later.

When people talk of the Mexico Inn, the memories include bean burros, topopo salads and chimichangas, but they also include Rachelle and Alfonso's warmth and generosity that were so much a part of the Mexico Inn.

Lloyd's

Lloyd's was a name that cropped up often when researching Mexican restaurants. It was located just south of the university on Sixth Street and was owned by Lloyd Vacovsky, a Czech American, with a boatload of recipes handed down to him from his first wife's aunt.[54]

Lloyd opened his humble little shop in 1953 and continued until sometime in the early 1980s, when the university took over the entire block. He closed every year for the month of August, which in Tucson was not unusual. One waitress named Charlotte was with Lloyd for nearly thirty years. Customers weren't just the college crowd, and everyone had their favorite: green chile, tacos and, as one customer remarked in a response to an article in the *Tucson Weekly* in March 2012, "the best enchiladas ever."[55]

Toward the end, hours were limited to weekday lunches, but Lloyd left behind a legacy in his cookbook, *Francisca's Mexican Cookbook*. Published in 1966 by Charles J. Merchant, the tiny softcover book is highly sought after by all the loyal customers of Lloyd's.

Gordo's Mexicateria & Mexicatessan

From an interview with Julie Valenzuela and Marguerite Brown, June 2015.

In 1963, Diego "Gordo" Valenzuela was a very successful life insurance salesman, but one evening, he packed his wife, Julie, and their two kids in the car and drove them to a corner on the west side of the town. He pulled into a lot with a small strip mall and announced to his family that he wanted to open a restaurant there. A few months later, armed with recipes from his mother-in-law's kitchen, he opened the doors to Gordo's Mexicateria & Mexicatessan.

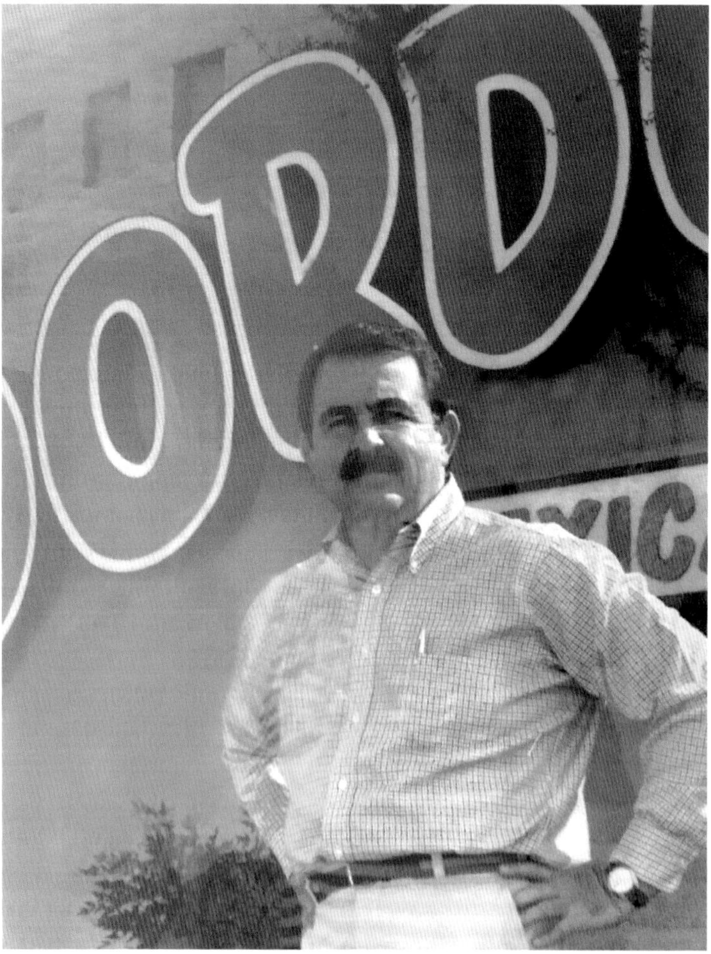

A young Gordo in front of his eponymous restaurant. *The Valenzuela family.*

"It was just a sliver of a restaurant," said his daughter, Marguerite. But Gordo didn't need much more than that.[56] Food was served cafeteria style because, according to Julie, Gordo didn't like to wait for his food, and he wanted people to feel like they were eating at a home, where you served yourself the food that was sitting on the stove.

But just because Gordo's was a cafeteria didn't mean Gordo cut corners. Every day, they would start fresh, using the "right" ingredients. "We didn't have cans," said Marguerite. "Literally we had people constantly cleaning beans. That's how fresh they were. Nothing was ever reheated. Any food that was left over at the end of the day was given to a food bank." Their original cook learned all the recipes, and before she retired, she taught them to a woman named Florence, who stayed with the business nearly to the end.

The restaurant was located just down the road from Flowing Wells High School, and so it soon became the local hangout at lunch time. On days when it rained, the street heading back to the school would flood (it wasn't called Flowing Wells for nothing), and Valenzuela would pack the kids into his big van and get them back to school in time for the next class.

Gordo loved kids, and he got to know many of them over the years. He knew when a kid didn't have money for lunch, and they never left the restaurant hungry. He gave them jobs, got to know their families and, in later years, helped them pay for college or buy a car. Marguerite noted that her father's generosity didn't just include teens. If someone couldn't pay, her folks made sure that they got something to eat. They never turned anyone away.

After a few years, he moved the restaurant up the street a bit and then moved to midtown. For a short time, the family had two restaurants operating at the same time. But it got to be too much work after the woman who ran the original place fell and broke her knee, so they closed the restaurant in the Flowing Wells area. From midtown, Gordo's moved farther east and eventually to the far eastside. There was even one in the university area. All in all, he had five restaurants in the forty-five years he was in business, each as popular as the next one.

But the flavors remained consistent, said Marguerite, thanks to the commitment to use the right ingredients and old-time methods.[57] One of the favorite dishes was the green chile con carne. Julie said that no one in town came close to duplicating it. And of course, there were Gordo's famous chimichangas.

Somewhere along the line, Valenzuela realized that he needed to advertise. Where he came up with the catchphrase he became famous for no one really knows, but Julie remembered him practicing in the shower. Gordo did all the

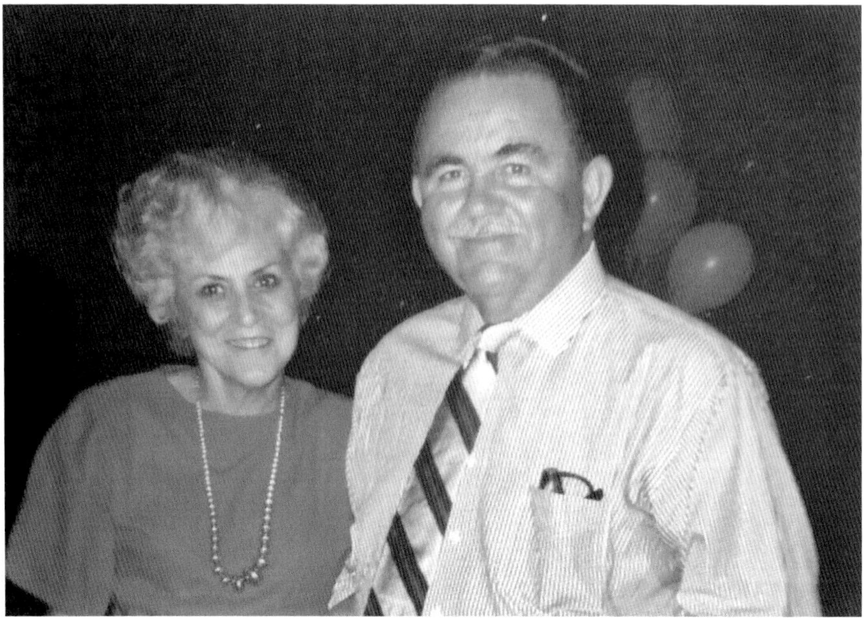

Julie and Gordo Valenzuela. *The Valenzuela family.*

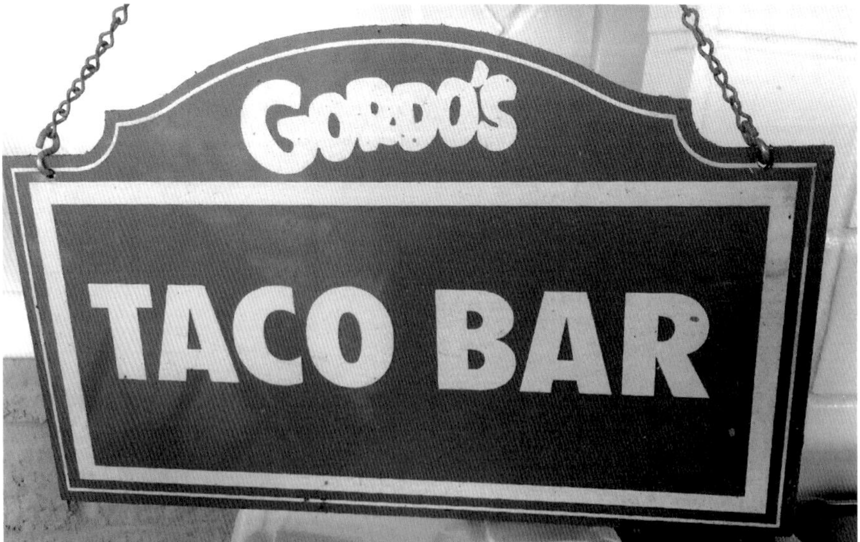

Tacos at Gordo's were good, too. *The Valenzuela family.*

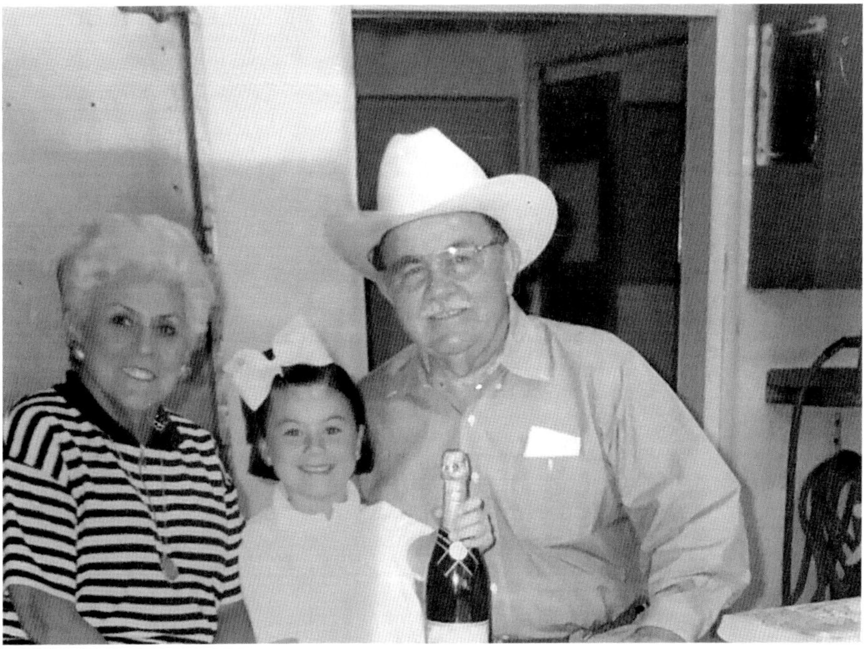

Julie, young Marguerite and Gordo Valenzuela celebrate. *The Valenzuela family.*

ads himself, and soon his smiling face and "If you like chimichangas. I mean if you *really* like chimichangas..." were more recognizable than the mayor.[58]

The number of chimis sold over all those years isn't known, but Marguerite estimated that the numbers were in the millions. Big chimis, mini chimis, chimis filled with green chile or red chile or refried beans—all were delicious. A manufacturing plant was necessary, and food was sold to both Costco and Fry's grocery stores with the Gordo's label.

Valenzuela wasn't just a clever businessman. He also gave back to the community. He served as president of the Arizona Historical Society. He helped found Casa de los Niños, Tucson's premier shelter for kids taken from abusive homes. He helped establish the Mountain Oyster Club, a private men's club. He owned radio stations and raised horses.

Gordo's was such a big part of so many people's lives. It served generations of people. Bob Hope ate there. Kids coming home from college were known to beg their parents take them directly to Gordo's from the airport. The Valenzuela family sold the restaurant in 2002. Two years later, the restaurant closed. The new owners just couldn't come close to meeting the standards set by Gordo and his family. Diego died in 2003.

"We had had wonderful, wonderful, wonderful people," said Julie. "We really made a dent for the forty-five years we were in business. People from all over the world knew about Gordo's and still ask about us," said Marguerite. "It was a part of history. Gordo's was such an iconic place that it was a part of Tucson history."

The Origin of the Chimichanga

Every Tucsonan knows that chimichangas originated in Tucson. Stories differ, but we consider any story that says the fried burrito was first made any place but the Old Pueblo to be nonsense.

One story, the one that most people know, credits Monica Flin, the woman who started El Charro, as the creator of the chimichanga.[59] El Charro is not one of Tucson's lost restaurants; in fact, it holds the title of the "nation's oldest Mexican restaurant in continuous operation by the same family." But this version has Monica cooking in her kitchen surrounded by her grandchildren. Apparently, she dropped a burrito in hot oil and began to use rather nasty Mexican cuss word but caught herself in time and shouted "Chimichanga!" instead.

The other story comes from the man who made chimichanga a household word, Diego "Gordo" Valenzuela. Gordo's certainly sold enough chimis in the forty-five years it was in business to lay claim to the title. This version

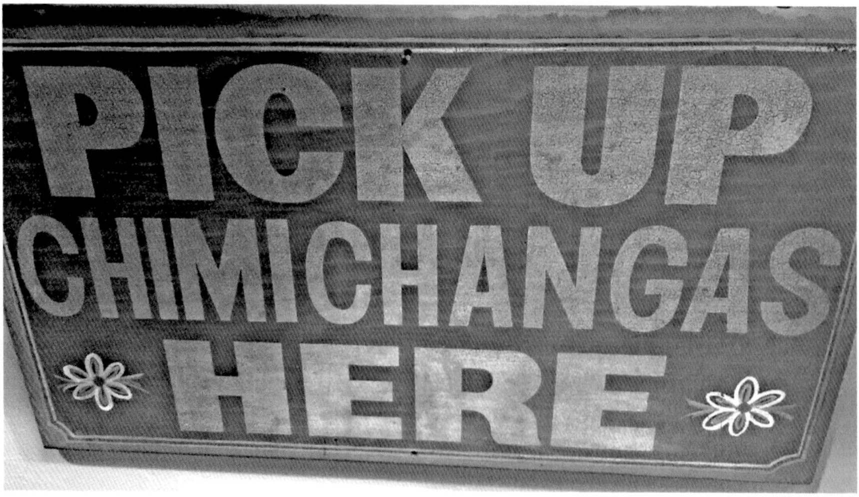

Get your chimis here. *The Valenzuela family.*

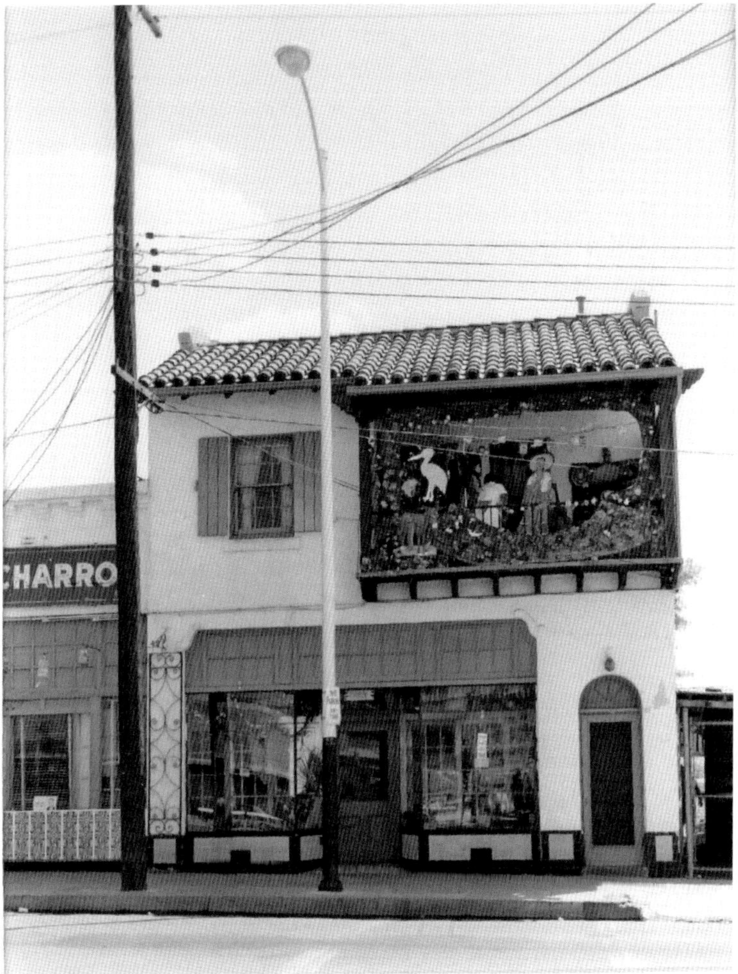

El Charro is not a closed restaurant, but this is the original El Charro, which was torn down in the name of progress. "El Charro Restaurant," 1965. *Walter L. Goodwin Jr., photographer. Commissioned by the Tucson Art Center. From the collection of the Tucson Museum of Art and Historic Block/Walter L. Goodwin Jr.*

has Gordo showing his new deep-fryer to a customer. The customer then asked if he could have a fried burrito. Gordo complied, and thus was born the chimichanga.

As far as the word itself goes, Tucson folklorist Dr. "Big Jim" Griffith thinks that it may have something more to do with the Mexican word for thingamajig, or something you've forgotten. Whichever the case, the chimichanga is a Tucson thing.

El Chaparral

Calling El Chaparral humble is an understatement. Stepping through the doors of the small adobe building, one was transported to a village in Mexico. The ceilings were low, a half dozen mismatched tables filled the tiny space, Christmas lights added a nice glow and beer brought in by customers was kept in the ancient refrigerator in the back room. The walls, though, held the paintings of local artist Ted DeGrazia, whose studio took up the rest of the grounds.[60]

Rosita was always there. In fact, she was the only person who ever seemed to be working there, serving up her humongous chimichangas and other made-to-order dishes with few words and a warm smile. The menus were handwritten on old Christmas cards. Chimichangas were a favorite here. No beer was served, but customers often brought their own. Rosita kept them cold in the little refrigerator in the back.

When the land was sold and the building torn down to build a gas station, Rosita moved two doors down. But the place had lost its charm, and Rosita was tired. It lasted only about two years in the new digs.

1970s

Papagayo

From an interview with Bryan and Alice Maezon, June 2015.

The decision to open a Mexican restaurant must've been an easy one for René Pérez Sr. After all, his family was one of the first families in Tucson. In the mid- to late 1800s, his grandfather Alex Levin owned and operated Levin's Garden, Tucson's main entertainment venue for many years. Levin also owned a series of saloons and a brewery.

René's mother, Sofia, ran La Conquista Mexican restaurant for forty years. He started there as the "ice breaker," which had nothing to do with warming up a crowd but more to do with using an ice pick to break up huge blocks of ice for drinks.[61] And his grandmother's family, the Molinas, also became known as one of Tucson's most famous restaurant families. So when he opened his family-style restaurant, Papagayo, in 1973, it was a natural decision.

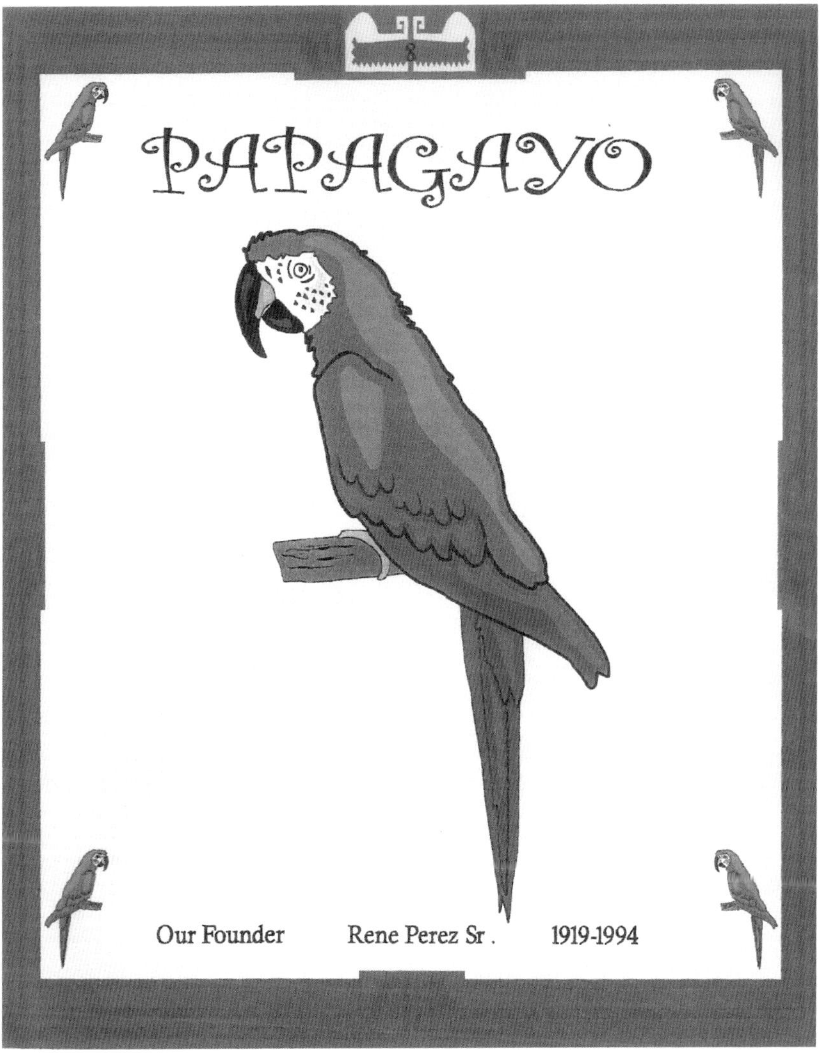

Papagayo means "parrot" in Spanish. Parrots could be found everywhere at the restaurant, including on the menu. *The Mezon family.*

Papagayo means "parrot" in Spanish, and René loved parrots. The colorful birds played a major role in décor. The birds were on murals, in the fountain and in bird cages throughout the two dining rooms. Other Mexican knickknacks and piñatas gave the place a bright, welcoming vibe. The patio was one of the best in town, with a bubbly fountain, tropical plants and a huge bush of bougainvillea.

Alice Mezon, his daughter, and Bryan Mezon, his grandson, brag about René's generosity when it came to the community and employees. He helped in the early days of Casa de Los Niños, Tucson's child abuse shelter. Every year, he'd close the restaurant for an evening and prepare a special menu charity dinner. He paid for employees' schooling. He purchased uniforms for entire baseball teams. And he was always willing to train employees in the fine art of hospitality.

The chiles rellenos were a specialty here. They were always made with fresh green chiles. The menu warned that "fresh chiles vary in intensity from season to season." Diner, beware![62] Other specialties included year-round green corn tamales, a rarity. René got the corn fresh from Mexico, and each tamale had good-sized strips of more of those fresh green chiles. People also liked the fajitas; the chicken ones were made with only white meat (the Mezons noted that only white meat was used in all chicken dishes). Just about every review of Papagayo also mentions the buñuelos, deep-fried tortillas enhanced with cinnamon and honey.

In 1989, the Pérezes opened a second restaurant in the foothills at Sunrise and Swan, with Alice in charge. It served the same food but to a fancier clientele. A third place on Tanque Verde Road, on Restaurant Row, was open for a short while. René died in 1993, but he never really left the restaurant. Employees used to tell Alice that on certain evenings they would hear the sound of someone jingling a set of keys, a habit for which René was famous.[63]

The Fort Lowell restaurant closed in 1996. Alice closed the Foothills venue in 2010.

The Old Adobe Patio

Although over time this place had changes in ownership and name, it's the name Old Adobe Patio that most people remember. Located in Broadway Boulevard in the heart of downtown, the outdoor seating could have been loud and uncomfortable. But the thick walls of the former Charles Brown House kept all traffic noises at bay. You could eat inside, but then you would miss the lush beauty of the "Patio."

Tall trees (some of which Brown had planted) shaded customers. Large bushy bougainvillea added splashes of color. Soft music played in the background. There was a feel of old Mexico, or at least Old Tucson. An evening on the Patio was relaxing and somewhat elegant.

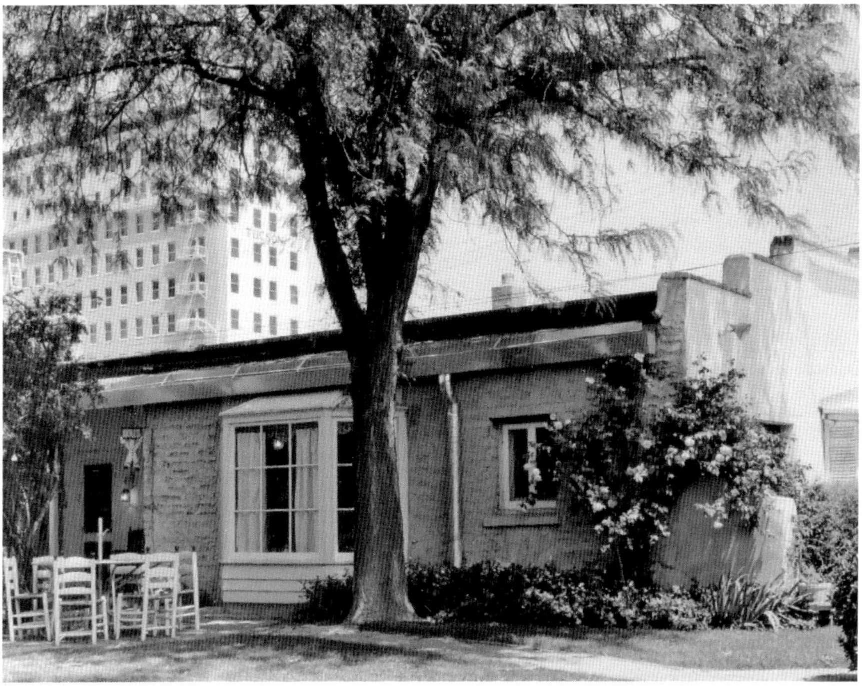

The Old Adobe Patio was once the home of Charles O. Brown, an early Tucson pioneer. *"Old Adobe Patio," Walter L. Goodwin Jr., photographer, 1965. Commissioned by the Tucson Art Center. From the collection of the Tucson Museum of Art and Historic Block.*

Charles O. Brown was an early pioneer in Tucson. Like many others, he made his fortune by owning a saloon. He was instrumental in the politics of territorial Arizona. Brown built the house in 1868 and spared no expense. The wood for the huge rafters, called *vigas*, was brought in by ox cart from the Santa Rita Mountains. He imported household goods from England. He had the first bathtub in the city installed in the house. All that attention to detail and use of the best materials paid off. The house was designated a historic property and maintained by the Arizona Historical Society (and owned by the state) for many years.

There were several small shops in the building as well, but it was the restaurant that attracted the crowds. The menu had a few American dishes (that number fluctuated depending on whoever was the owner), but the chiles rellenos always beat out the broiled chicken, and the sopa de albondigas (meatballs) beat out the French onion soup.[64]

If you couldn't make up your mind, there was the Old Adobe Comida Mexicana, a combination plate that held an enchilada, a taco, a chile relleno,

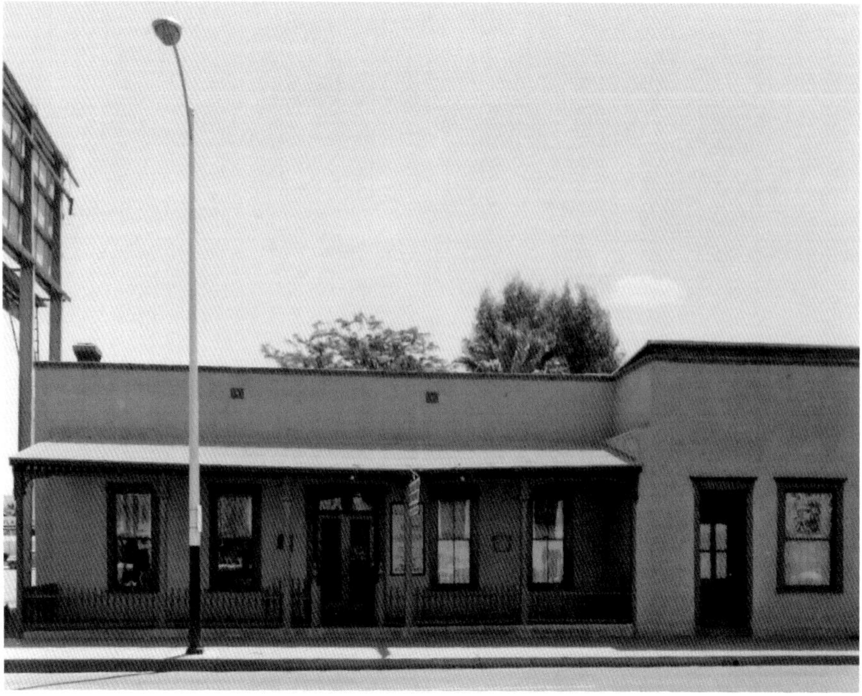

The front view of the Old Adobe Patio. *"Old Adobe Patio," Walter L. Goodwin Jr., photographer, 1965. Commissioned by the Tucson Art Center. From the collection of the Tucson Museum of Art and Historic Block.*

guacamole, a tostada, refried beans and rice. Flan was the finishing touch, although something called the Jamaica rum pie was "made famous at the Old Adobe."

In 1994, the Morris family, who had owned the restaurant for sixteen years, was given the order to vacate. The building was turned into El Centro Cultural de las Américas, headquarters for a Hispanic cultural group.[65] Today, Ben's Bells, a local charity, occupies the space. The patio is still there, even some of the trees, but any hints of the former restaurant are gone.

El Parador

The Jacobs family has been a part of the restaurant scene in Tucson for decades. Known for its Sonoran food and lovely garden-like setting (the Carousel Gardens was a previous incarnation), El Parador was a classic. But times and appetites changed. In 2014, Loretta Jacobs Carlson, David Jacobs

From an interview with Andrea Davis, July 2015.

The building at 2744 East Broadway Boulevard was home to El Parador for nearly forty years. But few people remember its original incarnation as Walter Hartwig's Carousel Gardens. Known as "Paris in the Desert," Carousel Gardens was the perfect place for ladies who lunch. It was "air-conditioned" and had an "impeccable cuisine" that was "planned and served under the esthetic and meticulous eye of Walter Hartwig." They could shop at one of the exclusive boutiques that circled the dining area and then sit down to a "fine" lunch and a fashion show.

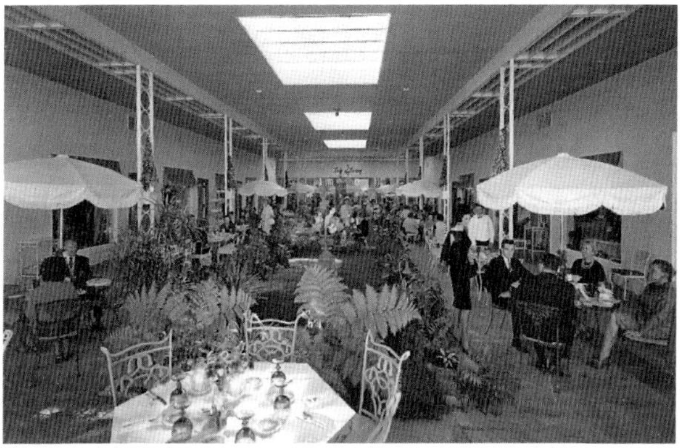

The Carousel Gardens later became El Parador. *From the collection of Dwight and Christy Schannep, American Antique Mall.*

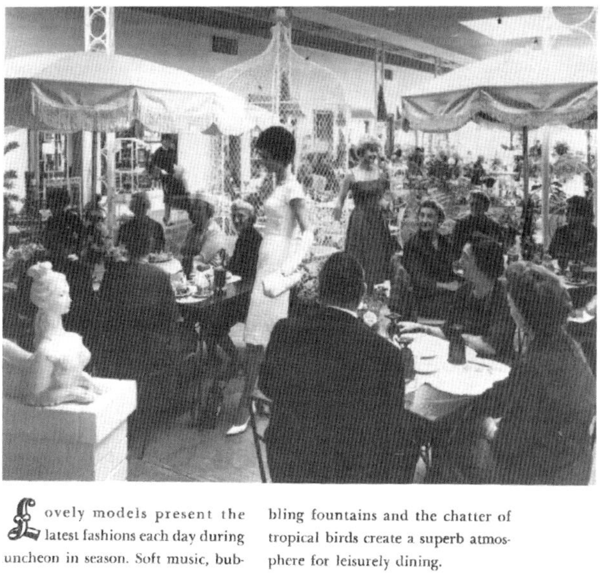

A lovely lunch at the Carousel Gardens. *Andrea Davis.*

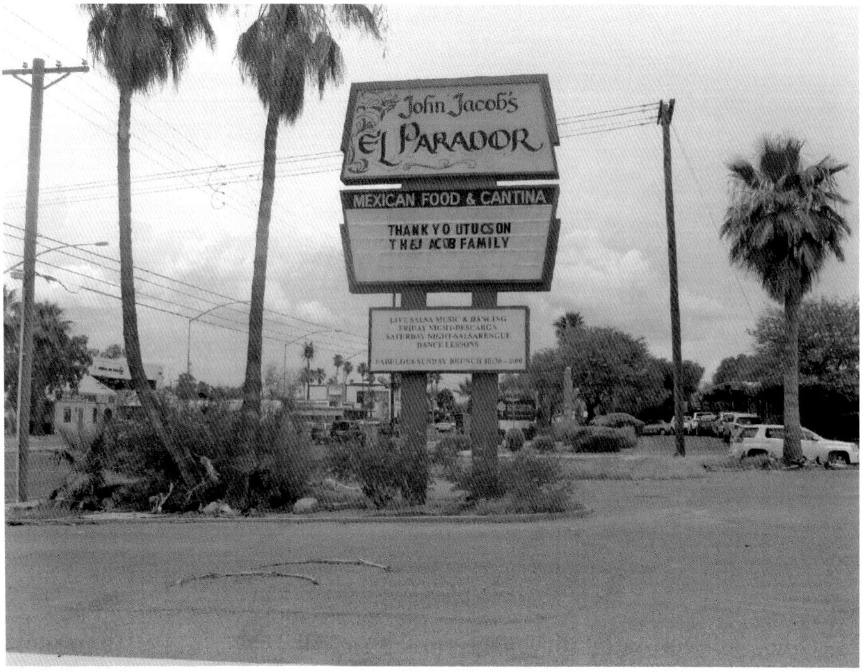

The Jacobs family says goodbye and thank you. *Author's collection.*

and Daniel Jacobs, children of the original owners, decided that it was time to try something different. The closure came as a surprise to people, many of whom had been dining there since early days.

Eating at El Parador was like eating in someone's lovely shaded garden, with skylights and lush foliage that even included rubber trees. The spot was known for its many house specialties and delicious margaritas.

Tia Elena's Ghost

Tia Elena's was owned and operated by the Corral family for many years. It was known for quality food, but dining at Tia Elena's was more like dining at an art museum. James Corral, the original owner, designed and made the metal and cement sculptures seen there. Many were of animals and such; others were free-form objects. The only remaining piece sits out front of the now empty building: a free-form

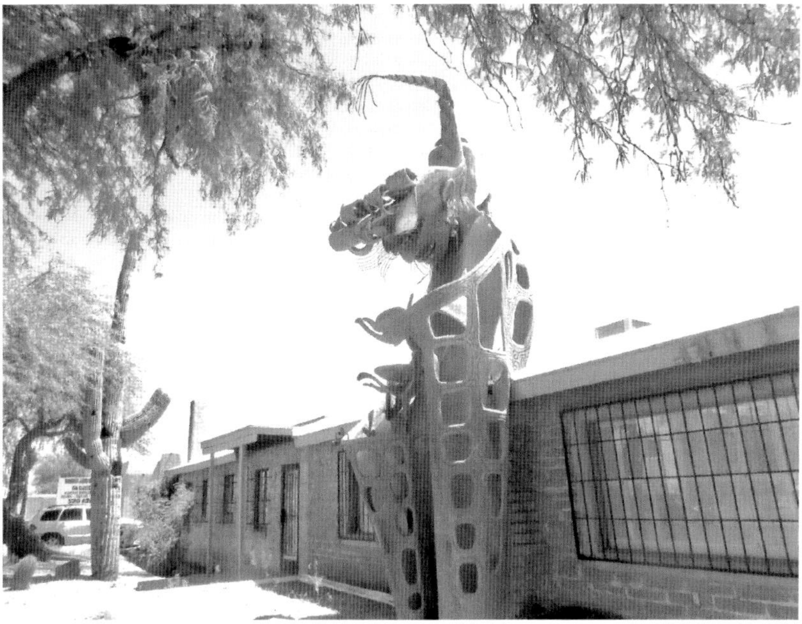

Tia Elena's is gone, but the *Iron Lady* still stands guard. *Author's collection.*

work of a woman who seems to be pouring water. Apparently, the statue served as a chimney, and when the restaurant was in operation, her eyes lit up.

But Tia Elena's is known for something else: a resident ghost. On and off during the years the restaurant was in business, both customers and employees saw and/or felt her presence. She seemed to be a friendly ghost, but nothing was ever really proven. After Tia Elena's closed, she was never heard from again by any of the businesses that occupied the building, according to the December 5, 1983 *Tucson Citizen*.

Chapter 3

Steakhouses and Western Flavors

You Gotta Have a Gimmick

From the 1940s to the 1970s, steakhouses were a big part of the dining scene in Tucson. Western beef, a baked potato, cowboy beans and warm dinner rolls were served pretty much the same at all of the various steakhouses, yet each restaurant was unique. Everyone had their favorite, and the regulars knew the other regulars as well as any of the staff. Live music was usually part of the scene. Sometimes there was dancing. OK Corral, the Baron's and the Ranchers Club were popular places, but the following spots were the ones that came to mind when someone would say, "Let's go out for a good steak."

The Pack 'Em Inn

The Pack 'Em Inn was located on the far eastern tip of Miracle Mile. It opened in 1964 and was the quintessential steakhouse. It was run by the Packham family: Everett, Mae and Tom.

The aroma of smoke hit you as you walked into the dimly lit main dining room. A small room sat off to the side, and there were a few small tables in the bar. There was lots of dark wood, a few booths and a host of wooden tables that sat bare. Compared to other nearby places—Ye Olde Lantern, for example—the prices were reasonable, and the décor was simple.

You had your choice of steaks, barbecue chicken and even some seafood options. There was also a house "steerburger" and prime rib on weekends. But what made the Pack 'Em Inn stand out among all the other steakhouses was that the cowgirl-dressed waitresses cooked all the steaks.

A huge open grill sat in the middle of the room, and after the server took your order, she'd prep a salad, deliver it to the table along with big fat sesame-seeded breadsticks and then plop your steak on the grill, keeping a careful eye on it while waiting other tables. It was hard work, and eventually the waitresses were relieved of kitchen duties. No one seemed to notice any major differences, except for maybe the waitresses.

The Packhams also owned the River Belle Saloon on North Oracle Road. The exterior of the building resembled an old-fashioned riverboat. The menus were similar, but the River Belle's menu concentrated more on seafood. The Pack 'Em Inn closed in 2007, and the building stands empty, much to the dismay of loyal customers.

The Hidden Valley Inn

There probably wasn't any more western-styled restaurant in Tucson than the Hidden Valley Inn. From the moment you pulled into the driveway, you knew what was in store. Huge covered wagons and a wishing well were prominently displayed out front. A sign proclaiming, "Howdy Partner, Welcome to the Hidden Valley Inn" stood in the entryway.

Inside was more of the same—way more. Saddles and lariats, bits and buckles, cowboy boots and hats, you name it—just about anything you might find on a ranch or in a western movie was part of the décor.[66]

The huge space was divided into three areas: the Crystal Palace, the entertainment venue; the Red Garter Saloon; and the immense dining room called the Hayloft. Seating was 360 people, and there was a waiting list on many nights.

In the hallway were the world-famous dioramas depicting western life. Carved miniature cowboys and cowgirls, horses, numerous buildings, a circus, a ghost town, an Indian village and Buffalo Bill's Wild West Show kept people—kids and grown-ups alike—entertained while they waited for their food. Words really can't describe the detail involved. The carvings were the work of former circus clown Jean LeRoy.

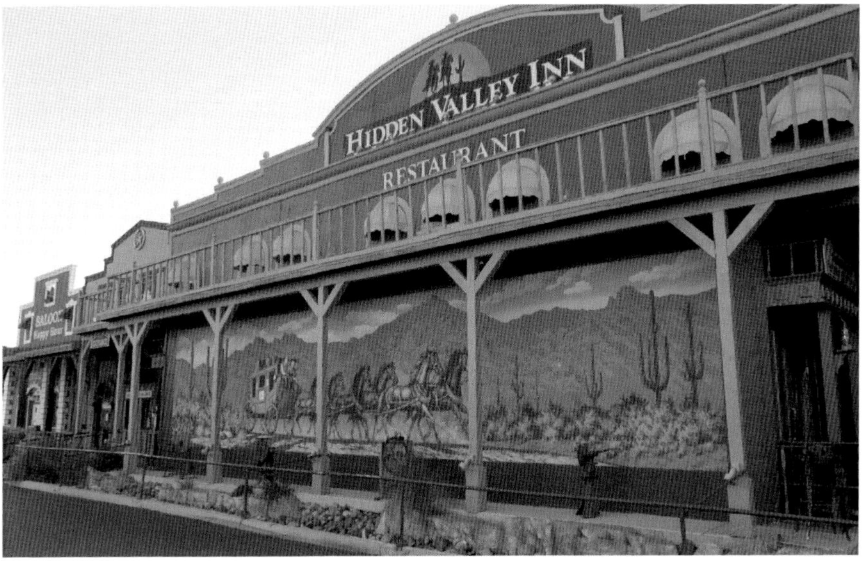

Hidden Valley Inn before the fire. *From the* Arizona Daily Star.

The building was once a stopover where local ranchers could enjoy a long cold one, and then it spent a short time as a German restaurant. For the majority of its existence, though, the Hidden Valley Inn was one of Tucson's premier steakhouses. Opened by the Colligan family in 1977, this was the place locals took visiting friends to give them a taste of the Old West. Larry Colligan Sr. (and his son, Larry Jr.) were familiar faces in Tucson thanks to the memorable television ads.

Red meat was the attraction, of course. The beef and pork was all corn-fed. Strip steaks, rib-eyes, T-bones, sirloin and filet mignon were all on the menu. So was prime rib in three sizes. And the ribs! Ah, the ribs were heavenly. The pork ribs were cooked over mesquite wood and slathered in the house hickory-smoked barbecue sauce. They were the epitome of what cowboy ribs should be. For a while, there was a delivery service called Mr. C's.[67]

Then, on August 7, 1995, a grease fire spread to the roof, and soon the entire place was ablaze.[68] All the western memorabilia was destroyed, but by luck, Colligan had removed much of the contents of the dioramas to be repaired, and the little village and all its citizens were spared.[69]

It took about a year to rebuild, with nearly double the seating, but soon the Hidden Valley Inn was back in business, this time with a sprinkler system. The Colligans sold the restaurant in 1997. The new owners ran it almost ten years before finally closing in 2006.

Gus & Andy's

Gus & Andy's was a mainstay of Miracle Mile for fifty-five years. The interior was dark and masculine. If busy Miracle Mile was right out the front door (which it was), no one really noticed. Gus & Andy's was all a product of the 1950s, with reds and blacks and wood everywhere.

This place was known for live music, lingerie fashion shows and red meat in all its glorious forms. Jimmy Gekas of the Palomino, which also was known for great steaks, noted that Gus & Andy's probably had the best prime rib in town.[70] Gus & Andy's attracted a mix of customers: local businessmen, football coaches, movie stars (whose photos lined the hallways) and even a mobster or two.

Gus and Andy Lettas, two brothers of Greek heritage, were owners and operators. Their sister, Kathryn, was also part of the mix. They opened in 1949.[71] The live music was usually jazz and lasted until just before the place closed. A statuette of Louis Armstrong provided inspiration.

People went to Gus & Andy's because it never really changed. It was reliable, comfortable and affordable until its closing day in 2004.

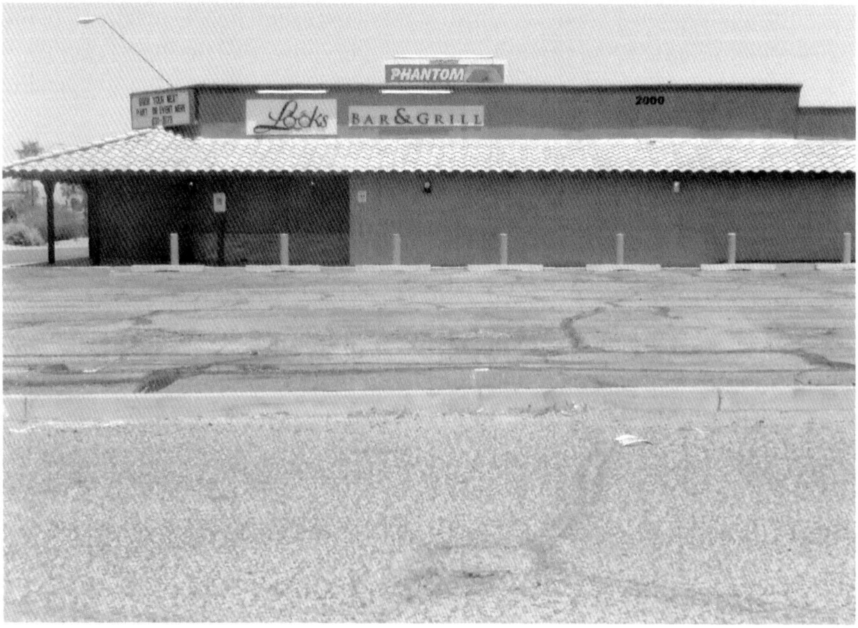

Gus & Andy's is now the Lookout Lounge. *Author's collection.*

TRIPLE C CHUCKWAGON

The Triple C was probably more popular with visitors than it ever was with locals. It was the epitome of what those greenhorns from back east imagined Tucson to be, minus the rattlesnakes and stagecoach-robbing bandits.

This western-style eatery was located far west of town on Bopp Road, and dinner was served in a huge barn-like building. Servers were dressed in cowboy/cowgirl regalia. When that dinner bell rang, upward of 550 people sat down to a dinner of western-style beef in barbecue sauce, cowboy beans, baked potatoes wrapped in aluminum foil, biscuits with butter and jelly and spiced peaches. Everything was made from scratch, according to the brochure.[72]

Run by the Camp family (Chuck, Mae, Shelly, Bill and Cathy), the Triple C was open from November to May (peak tourist season in these parts) and featured a live musical show. The Camps did much of the entertaining themselves, but the big draw was the Sons of the Pioneers, the six-man singing group that set the standard for good old-fashioned western music.

Charles had come to Tucson in 1969 and worked various positions until opening the Triple C in 1971. He and the family ran it until his death in 2003. When the Triple C closed, the Sons of the Pioneers moved to the Hidden Valley Inn.

Chapter 4

From Fine Dining to Not-So-Nouvelle Cuisine

For several years in the mid- to late 1990s, the *Tucson Citizen* awarded the Silver Spoon Awards to the top-ten restaurants in the city. There were repeated winners over time, but it is interesting to note that of the Silver Spoon winners in 1997, only two restaurants survive. Tastes change, of course, but it is still sad to see that so many popular and successful restaurants are now lost.

Rossi's

Tucson has always been a casual sort of place, but that doesn't mean fine dining didn't exist. In fact, almost from the beginning of the real restaurants in the Old Pueblo, "people of refinement" could find elegant dining options. The Palace Hotel had a large dining room and boasted outstanding service and a large menu. But it was another freestanding restaurant that brought a true sense of fine dining to the city. Many restaurants came and went in early Tucson, but one that persevered into the twentieth century was Rossi's.

Opened by Alex Rossi and Gabriel Roletti, it was first called the Columbia and stood on the corner of what is now Stone Avenue and Congress Street.[73] The saloon opened in 1887 or so and had a little restaurant out back. By 1900, the food had become the major draw, and expansion was necessary. Thus, in 1900 the Columbia opened and met with great success from day

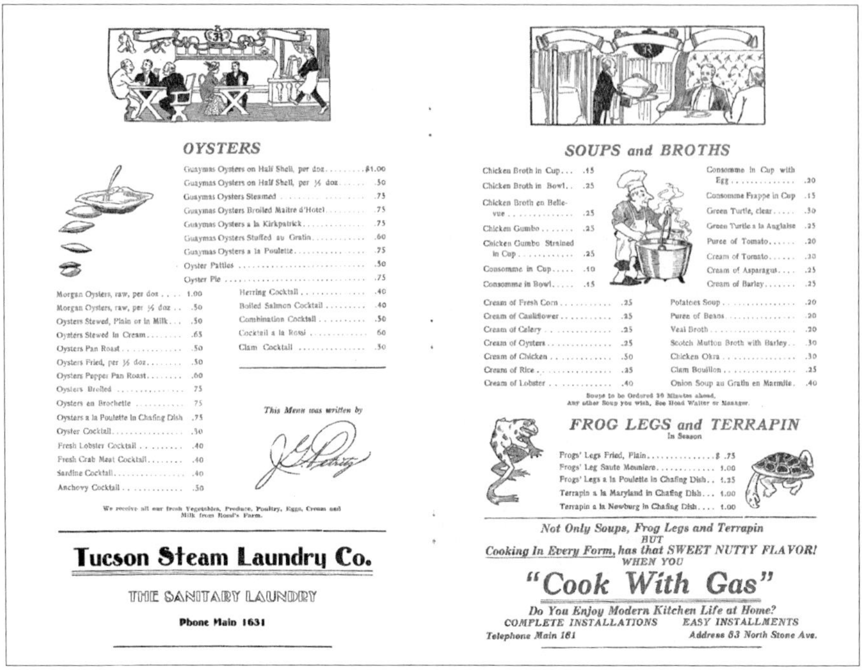

OYSTERS

Guaymas Oysters on Half Shell, per doz	$1.00
Guaymas Oysters on Half Shell, per ½ doz	.50
Guaymas Oysters Steamed	.75
Guaymas Oysters Broiled Maitre d'Hotel	.75
Guaymas Oysters a la Kirkpatrick	.75
Guaymas Oysters Stuffed au Gratin	.60
Guaymas Oysters a la Poulette	.75
Oyster Patties	.50
Oyster Pie	.75
Morgan Oysters, raw, per doz	1.00
Morgan Oysters, raw, per ½ doz	.50
Oysters Stewed, Plain or in Milk	.50
Oysters Stewed in Cream	.65
Oysters Pan Roast	.50
Oysters Fried, per ½ doz	.50
Oysters Pepper Pan Roast	.60
Oysters Broiled	75
Oysters en Brochette	75
Oysters a la Poulette in Chafing Dish	.75
Oyster Cocktail	.30
Fresh Lobster Cocktail	.40
Fresh Crab Meat Cocktail	.40
Sardine Cocktail	.40
Anchovy Cocktail	.50
Herring Cocktail	.40
Boiled Salmon Cocktail	.40
Combination Cocktail	.50
Cocktail a la Rossi	60
Clam Cocktail	.30

This Menu was written by

We receive all our fresh Vegetables, Produce, Poultry, Eggs, Cream and Milk from Rossi's Farm.

Tucson Steam Laundry Co.

THE SANITARY LAUNDRY

Phone Main 1631

SOUPS and BROTHS

Chicken Broth in Cup	.15
Chicken Broth in Bowl	.25
Chicken Broth en Bellevue	.25
Chicken Gumbo	.25
Chicken Gumbo Strained in Cup	.25
Consomme in Cup	.10
Consomme in Bowl	.15
Consomme in Cup with Egg	.20
Consomme Frappe in Cup	.15
Green Turtle, clear	.30
Green Turtle a la Anglaise	.25
Puree of Tomato	.20
Cream of Tomato	.20
Cream of Asparagus	.25
Cream of Barley	.25
Cream of Fresh Corn	.25
Cream of Cauliflower	.25
Cream of Celery	.25
Cream of Oysters	.25
Cream of Chicken	.50
Cream of Rice	.25
Cream of Lobster	.40
Potatoes Soup	.20
Puree of Beans	.20
Veal Broth	.20
Scotch Mutton Broth with Barley	.30
Chicken Okra	.30
Clam Bouillon	.25
Onion Soup au Gratin en Marmite	.40

Soups to be Ordered 30 Minutes ahead.
Any other Soup you wish, See Head Waiter or Manager.

FROG LEGS and TERRAPIN
In Season

Frogs' Legs Fried, Plain	$ .75
Frogs' Leg Saute Meuniere	1.00
Frogs' Legs a la Poulette in Chafing Dish	1.25
Terrapin a la Maryland in Chafing Dish	1.00
Terrapin a la Newburg in Chafing Dish	1.00

Not Only Soups, Frog Legs and Terrapin
BUT
Cooking In Every Form, has that SWEET NUTTY FLAVOR!
WHEN YOU

"Cook With Gas"

Do You Enjoy Modern Kitchen Life at Home?
COMPLETE INSTALLATIONS EASY INSTALLMENTS
Telephone Main 161 Address 83 North Stone Ave.

Pages two and three of Rossi's menu. The whole menu was eleven pages long. *Arizona Historical Society.*

one. After another expansion and a fancy upgrade, the restaurant was dubbed Rossi's.

Alex Rossi was an Italian immigrant who had spent time in the great kitchens of Europe and America. Roletti, somewhat of a silent partner, bowed out somewhere along the line, leaving Rossi to run the restaurant and saloon the way he wanted. And run it he did.[74]

Everyone was welcome at Rossi's. And although there probably isn't anyone around anymore that ever ate there, by all reports it was the social center of the city.

Rossi was known as an affable and honest man with a great sense of hospitality. On the inside front cover of the beautifully designed menu, he wrote, "Our object is to have you enjoy your meal in comfort. Therefore any inattention on the part of the employees should be reported."[75]

He raised many of the items in the menu on his farm outside town.[76] He also had an eye for detail, as was evident in the menu. More than eleven pages long, it was filled with a wide assortment of dishes. Categories included "Rarebit," "Cheeses," "Salads," "Omelets and

Sweet Omelettes," "Frogs Legs and Terrapin," "Soups," "Steaks" and "Diverses" (aka offal). There were Italian specialties as well: spaghetti Italian style, ravioli and risotto Milanaise, which required a two-hour notice. There was plenty of wine, beer and mixed drinks. And as if all that wasn't enough, the menu proclaimed, "We will prepare your favorite dish if it's not on the menu."[77]

Rossi ran the place with flair until just after Prohibition. On the last night before the Volstead Act went into effect, Rossi threw the party of the century, inviting everyone in town. They drank the place dry.[78] Rossi's closed in 1920 after the big bash. Rossi himself closed the doors for good and moved to Mexico. He died in 1930 at the age of seventy.

The Tack Room

From an interview with Drew and Kandie Vactor, July 2015.

The Tack Room is probably the one restaurant that everyone I talked with said should be included in this book. Even if they had never eaten at this iconic restaurant, people knew what it meant to Tucson culinary history.

The land on which The Tack Room was built sits along the Tanque Verde Wash, which at one time was a lush and flowing waterway. Seasonal flooding was not unusual. Framed by the majestic Santa Catalina and Rincon Mountain Ranges, the views of the Rincon Valley were stunning. It was the ideal spot to relax and have fun, and Robinson Carr Locke built a home there. He also built a horse racing track, thus establishing it as a site of entertainment and hospitality.

Then, in 1946, Marvin Kratter convinced a group of four to invest in the land and develop a guest ranch. Although the project eventually went bankrupt, one couple—Marvin Kane and his wife, Fan, who lived in Ohio—picked up the reins and opened Rancho del Rio.

Conveniently, their son, Jud, was going to school in Tucson, and they convinced him to take over management. He didn't want to be bothered with food service, so he called his sister, Alma Vactor, who was then living in Ohio, to take care of that end of the business. She along with husband David and three children moved to Tucson to take over managing all aspects of the ranch.

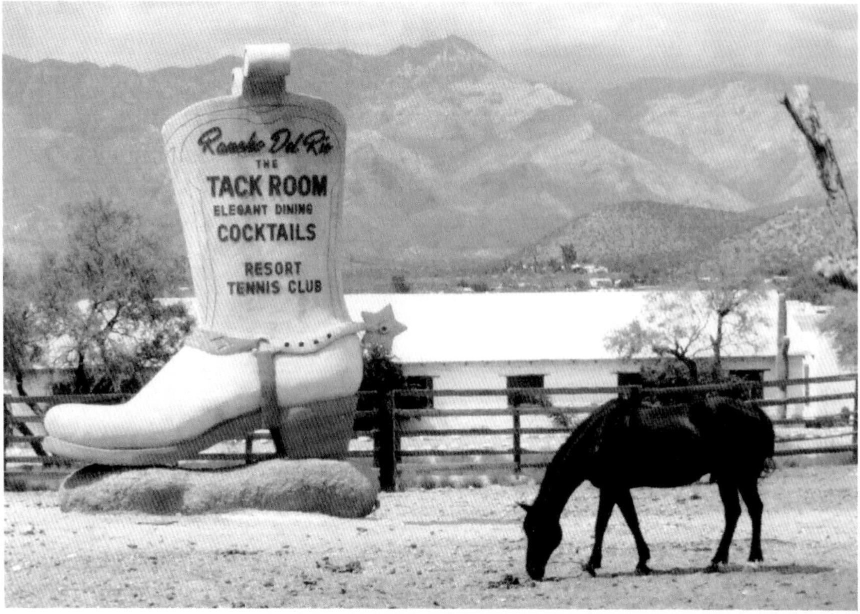

A shot of the Big Boot. *Drew and Kandie Vactor.*

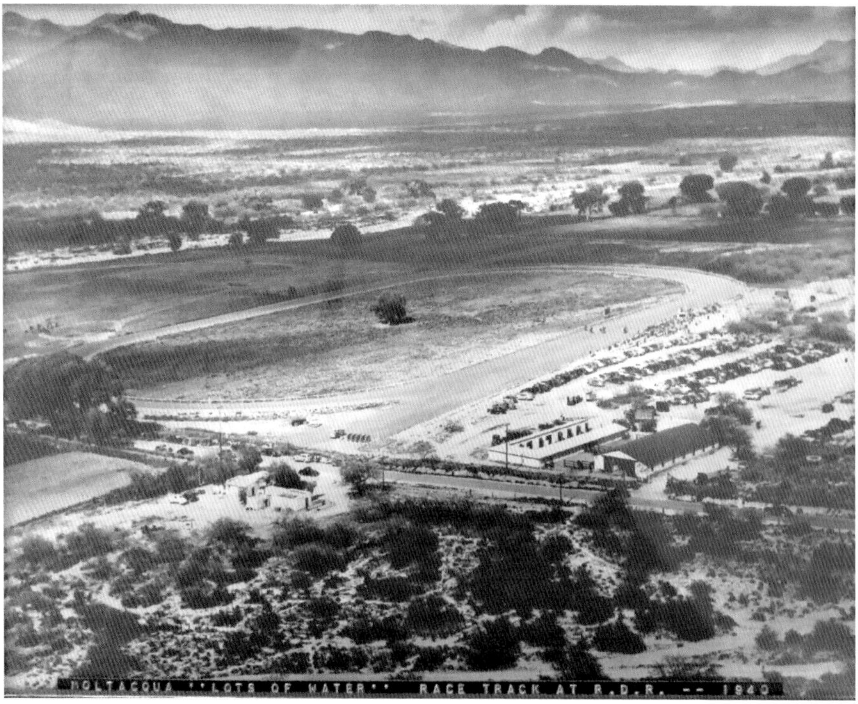

Aerial view of Rancho del Rio, circa 1940. *Drew and Kandie Vactor.*

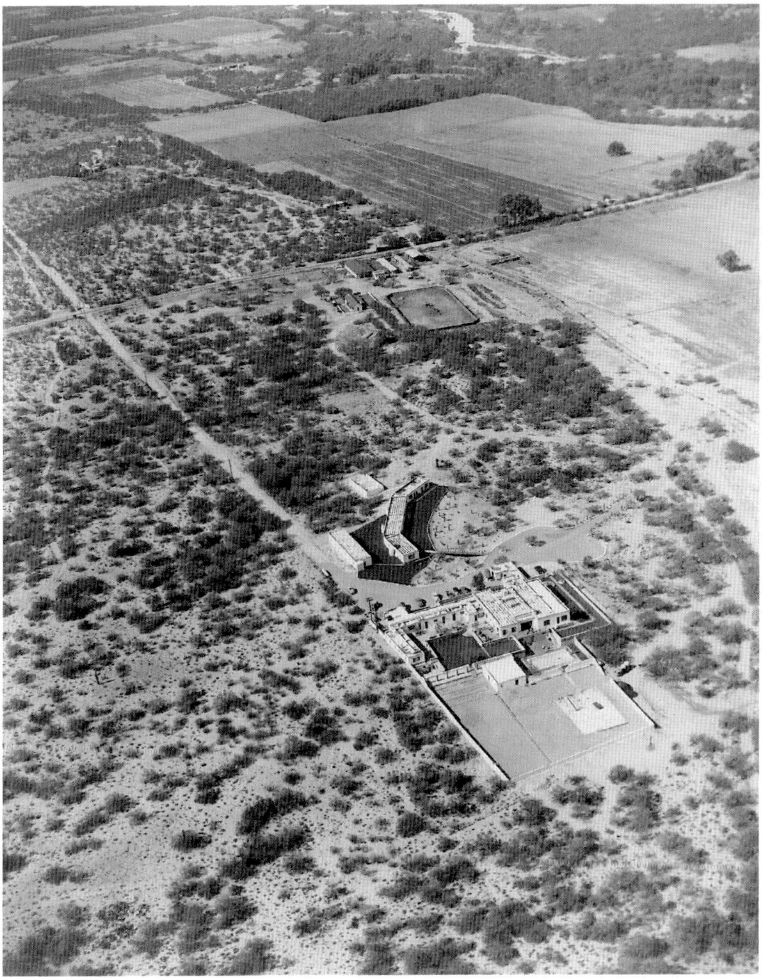

Rancho del Rio, 1950. *Drew and Kandie Vactor.*

The Vactor family grew up on the ranch. Son Drew, who later would be the driving force behind The Tack Room's growth, said, "In the winter, we'd share our home with one hundred people at a time, just like everyone does." But the family had to be practical. Running a guest ranch from mid-November to mid-May didn't cover all the yearly costs. David had a small runway that was used by the National Fire Service and grew alfalfa on half of the two-hundred-acre property, but still something more was needed.

This was in the 1960s, and there were no fine dining restaurants in the entire state of Arizona. The solution was simple: the Vactors would fill that niche, and The Tack Room opened its doors on January 27, 1965. It was an immediate success. People came from all around the state and then from all over the world to enjoy Alma's recipes in a rustically elegant setting, complete with those stunning views that had drawn the original owners to the land.

Along with the guests came accolades galore. In 1973, The Tack Room was the first Arizona restaurant to garner a Mobile Travel Guide Four Star Award. In 1977, it won the first of nineteen consecutive Mobile Five Star Awards. The first year AAA started rating restaurants, it won the 5 Diamond Award. The Tack Room was the only restaurant in the western United States to hold both titles for the first three years that it was possible to do so.

But as full as the walls of The Tack Room were with plaques proclaiming their excellence, that wasn't what kept the Vactors (Drew and wife Kandie) going. "It was about what the staff did to make it possible. It took a lot of people putting their heart and soul in it to make what we did possible."

In the early days, Charles Kerr—who would later open his own fine dining establishment, Charles—was the maître d'. Drew Vactor said that he learned everything he knows about service from Kerr. Richard Tyler was another important piece. He worked for many years as general manager and eventually became part owner.

The outstanding servers, all male, were dressed in tuxedos. Dishes would be flambéed and carved tableside. Empty glassware and dishes were whisked off the table, almost unnoticed. Guests felt like royalty and enjoyed some of the best food in the city. The menu was tweaked over the years, said Vactor. When the doors opened, the menu was all "haute cuisine," with the most expensive item being a steak at $8.95.

Drew began managing in 1974 when Jud died. He brought a youthful energy, a marketing/management degree and, of course, years of experience in knowing what made people happy. Drew and Kandie traveled around the United States with the purpose of seeing what other restaurants were doing. They were impressed by Mark Miller and his use of local ingredients for southwestern flavors. They didn't want to do too spicy but still wanted to preserve those unique flavors.

Their steak au poivre seemed a likely place to start. Instead of cracked black pepper on top, they used a blend of local chiles. From there, they revved up the traditional rack of lamb, turning the tired old mainstay into a memorable meal. They did keep some of the dishes that made The Tack Room famous. Vactor said that the menu was about half new/half traditional, and both sold equally well.

Most everyone who worked at The Tack Room started washing dishes and worked their way up. Some stayed in the kitchen; others moved to the front of the house. Either way, many people stayed there for decades because the Vactors treated them so well. The Vactors even worked out a plan whereby during the slow summer months, staff had jobs at a resort in Colorado. At the end of summer, they would fly those workers back to Tucson.

Plenty of stories came out of The Tack Room. Some, like getting engaged, were private and personal. Others, like the night Mo Udall entertained a large group of people from both Mexico and the United States, became legend. Vactor said that Udall had his guests rolling in the aisles.

While the dress code was "casual," no jeans, shorts, T-shirts or beach shoes were allowed. This policy was tested one evening when a woman, who was a regular, noticed a man with his back to the room dressed in blue jeans and a denim jacket. She called Vactor over and voiced her displeasure, commenting loudly that the standards had certainly dropped. Vactor told her that he would let Steve McQueen know. The woman then asked for McQueen's autograph.

When asked why he thought The Tack Room was so successful for so long, Vactor credited his staff, "They were the secret to what we did as a restaurant.

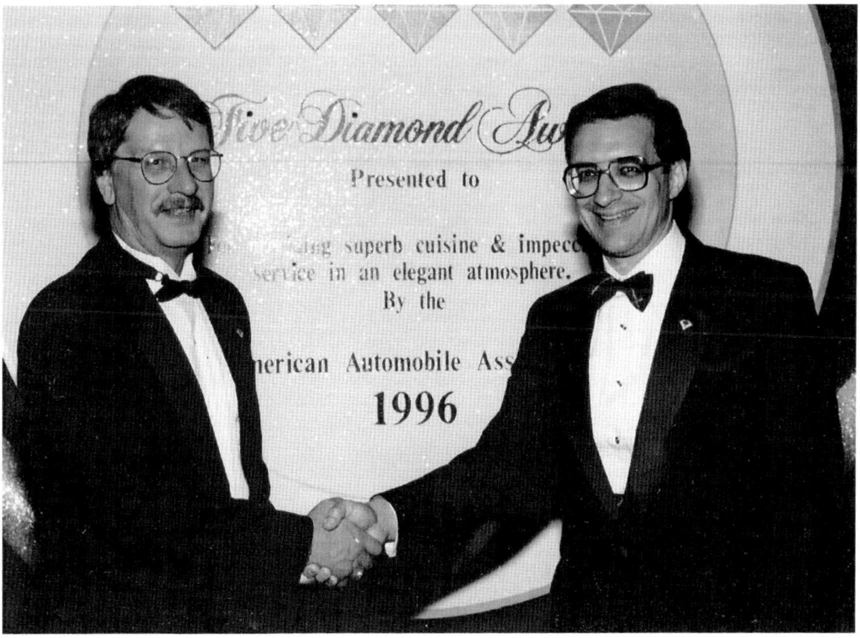

Drew Vactor's "5 Diamond" handshake when The Tack Room got its first five-star rating from AAA. *Kandie and Drew Vactor.*

It was a team effort. No one person was indispensable, but it was also a lot of different people doing a great job with the roles they played."

That's why it was so important to him that when he knew it was time for him to leave the business, he would make sure all those people were rewarded. He took two years to hammer out a plan, and then he found the perfect buyer in Bob McMahon. McMahon and Vactor's relationship went back to the early days of McMahon's company, City Meats. McMahon had just sold the company for a tidy sum and was looking to get into the restaurant business. They signed a five-year lease with the clause that the current staff would be retained. The Tack Room lasted about three more years. McMahon closed it down, paying the entire rent for five years.

These days, the Big Boot still acts as a sign, but for a gated community. Alma is still around, and Kandie and Drew keep busy traveling all over the world on cruise ships (they worked for many years teaching computer classes on cruise ships). Drew is an active member in a local Rotary group; Kandie is an honorary member. They along with countless guests have many wonderful memories of the legendary Tack Room. Dinner there was always a special occasion even if you weren't celebrating a special occasion.

The Gekas Family

From an interview with Kiki Kinkade, Genie Patterson and Jimmy Gekas, June 2015.

For more than five decades, the Gekas family entertained legions of Tucsonans in their various restaurants. Beginning in the late 1940s and continuing through the mid-'90s, Mary, John, their children and an assortment of cousins, siblings and family friends served elegant meals in elegant settings, ensuring that customers walked away happy and well fed.

A son of Greek immigrants, John moved to Tucson in 1937. After working at several local clothing stores, he decided to open the Flame Room with his cousin, John Paulos. Located at the corner of Congress Street and Church Avenue, the Flame Room was popular, bringing in people from all over the city to downtown.[79]

Then, in 1942, John took over a shabby little spot on the edge of town called Venice Gardens. He spiffed the place up and renamed it the Palomino after the many neighboring palomino ranches. He sold the place in 1948. Prior to that time, John had met a charming young woman named Mary

Sfarnas at his brother's wedding in his native Pennsylvania. He was smitten but returned to Tucson to keep the business running. Every night after the restaurant closed, John would write long love letters to Mary trying to convince her to marry him and move to Tucson. Eventually, he won her heart, and they were married in 1947.[80]

In 1954, the Flame Room burned down. John and John Paulos then opened Talk of the Town. The two spilt after a short while; Paulos opened Paulos' on East Speedway, and John opened several of places along Oracle Road. The first was Sirloin & Saddle, "Where the West Eats the Best." Here, according to an advertisement, the beef was western barley fed, and diners could enjoy their favorite cocktails in a "Southwestern atmosphere filled with melodious music nightly." Dinners started at $1.75. His brother-in-law, Jimmy Sfarnas, was co-owner and manager.[81] The Cliff House, which followed, soon became known for fine Continental dining and outstanding views of the city. It was located on Oracle Road, which was the main route to Phoenix before I-10 was built.

John hired Chef Otto Diemer, one of only nine Black Hat chefs in America. German-born and classically trained, Diemer created menus featuring sauces, soups, entrées and desserts prepared in the finest Continental style. On any given day, three stocks simmered on the stove. Sauces were created with a flick of cream here and a pat of butter there. The four mother sauces were made daily.[82] Diemer ran a tight ship, but the front of the house was no different. The maître d' conducted daily inspections of the staff. Woe betide to the busboy whose shoes weren't shined just so.

The Cliff House closed in the early '60s, and the Gekas clan moved on to the Coat of Arms farther up the road. The Coat of Arms was tucked well into the back of Casas Adobes Plaza on Oracle Road and had earned a reputation for fine English food, but a decision was made to change it over to a more Mediterranean style. Again, like all the others, the Coat of Arms met with huge success due to excellent food and gracious service. But then, in 1968, the landlord from the Palomino called asking to see if John and Mary had any interest in reopening the Palomino. Thankfully for Tucsonans, they said yes.

The interior was a wreck, with garish colors and shabby equipment. Mary stepped up to the plate. She had murals of palomino horses painted on the walls. They added black leather booths, tables and chairs and plush red carpeting.[83] The Coat of Arms was sold in 1972. The Palomino was then their only business. And it was with the Palomino that the Gekas family made their legacy.

The kitchen was run by Joe Giliardi, who during the war had been General Eisenhower's private chef. Mary did the baking—her famous cheese pie was

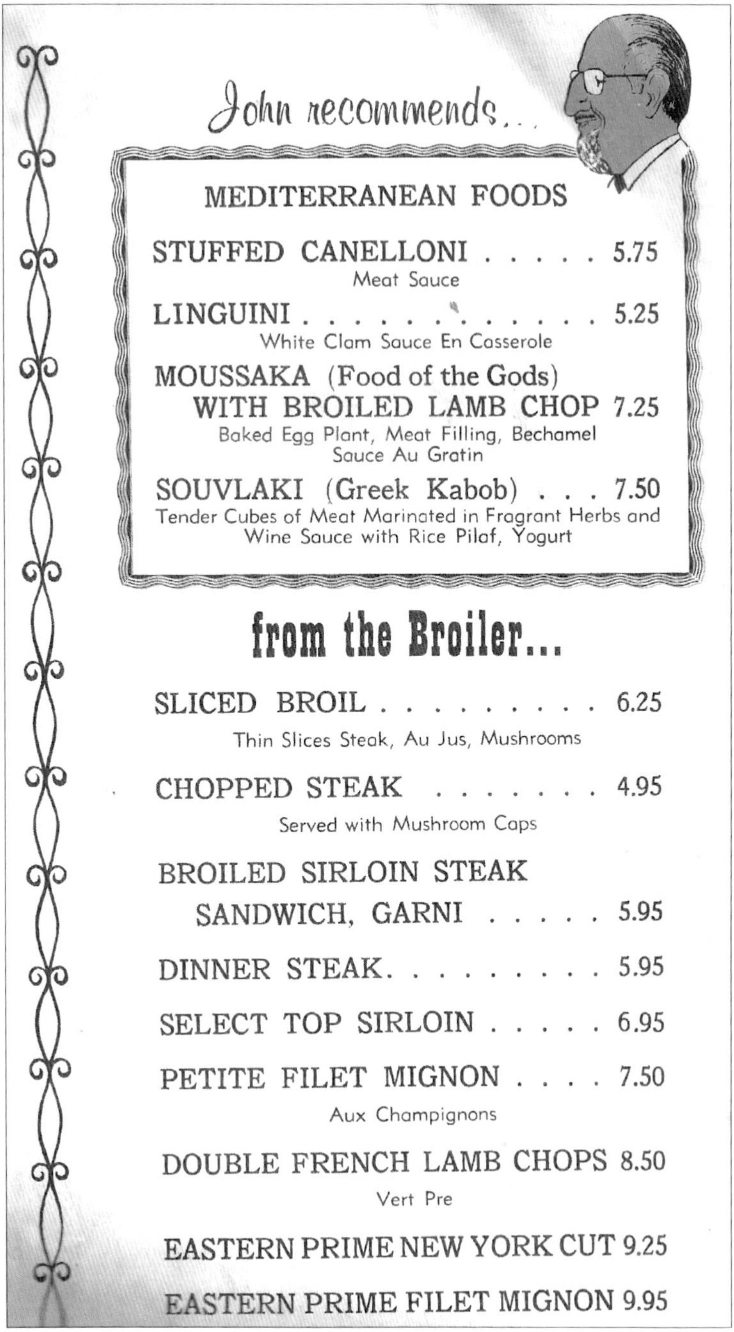

John recommends...

MEDITERRANEAN FOODS

STUFFED CANELLONI 5.75
Meat Sauce

LINGUINI 5.25
White Clam Sauce En Casserole

MOUSSAKA (Food of the Gods)
WITH BROILED LAMB CHOP 7.25
Baked Egg Plant, Meat Filling, Bechamel
Sauce Au Gratin

SOUVLAKI (Greek Kabob) . . . 7.50
Tender Cubes of Meat Marinated in Fragrant Herbs and
Wine Sauce with Rice Pilaf, Yogurt

from the Broiler...

SLICED BROIL 6.25
Thin Slices Steak, Au Jus, Mushrooms

CHOPPED STEAK 4.95
Served with Mushroom Caps

BROILED SIRLOIN STEAK
SANDWICH, GARNI 5.95

DINNER STEAK. 5.95

SELECT TOP SIRLOIN 6.95

PETITE FILET MIGNON 7.50
Aux Champignons

DOUBLE FRENCH LAMB CHOPS 8.50
Vert Pre

EASTERN PRIME NEW YORK CUT 9.25

EASTERN PRIME FILET MIGNON 9.95

The Palomino was the epitome of fine dining for more than twenty-five years. *The Gekas family.*

one of many other treats. Tuxedoed waiters prepared dishes such as the shrimp Napoli and flaming cherries jubilee tableside. Regulars had their favorite cocktails delivered to the table before they even had to ask. A night at the Palomino was always memorable.

Luminaries who dined at the Palomino included everyone from George C. Scott to Willie Nelson and President Gerald Ford to Joe Garagiola. When Paul Newman ate there, he arrived driving a bright yellow Corvette. Actor Robert Mitchum and his entourage, after a well-placed warning by Joe, were kicked out for swearing.[84]

Your signature was good enough. Son Jim said that probably about 40 percent of customers had house accounts. They could come in, have dinner and drinks and then merely sign the check, knowing that they'd be billed at the end of the month.

The whole family worked there. The kids—Jimmy, Kiki and Genie—started as dishwashers at an early age and learned all the stations so they could fill in should someone not show for work. Joe talked with the customers and made sure that the kitchen was on top of things. But it was Mary who was the heart of the Palomino. Mary was known for her slash of red lipstick, her gracious

The Gekas Family's Melitzansalata (Eggplant Dip)

1 large eggplant
1 onion, chopped
2 garlic cloves, crushed
1 tablespoon wine vinegar
1 tablespoon chopped parsley
½ cup olive oil

Preheat oven to 350 degrees. Puncture eggplant with a knife in 3 or 4 places to prevent from exploding while it bakes. Place eggplant in baking dish and bake for 1 hour. The skin will be wrinkled and soft to the touch. Cool for 10 minutes, scoop out the flesh of the eggplant and place in a blender. Add all the remaining ingredients into the blender and blend well. Chill until ready to serve with pita bread or any vegetable for dipping.

From *Greek Cooking: Recipes and Stories of My Greek Family* (2015).

hospitality, her open heart and her firm hand. Everyone has a wonderful story or two about Mary. Former busboys talk of how she was both boss and mother to them, teaching them the values of hard work and caring about others.[85]

Daughter Kiki recounted a conversation she had with a former busboy. One night there was a serious accident on the corner in front of the restaurant. He remembered Mary dropping everything to help and in doing so instilled in him a passion for emergency care. He became a firefighter somewhere back east.[86]

After John died in 1982, Mary—along with son Jimmy, who cooked—made sure that the tradition of the Palomino continued. Mary could be tenacious in dealing with the city leaders when issues arose, but she was also famous for her generosity. On one occasion she opened the restaurant on a Sunday (the Palomino was always closed on Sunday) for an on-the-spot fundraiser for a needy family.[87] And she was a huge patron of the arts. The Arizona Opera was a special favorite.[88]

Then, in 1994, the Gekas family closed the Palomino. Longtime customers were heartbroken. The Palomino had been where they'd gotten engaged or celebrated a promotion or, most often, had enjoyed many wonderful evenings with no special occasion needed.

Daughter Genie Patterson wrote a cookbook, *Greek Cooking: Recipes and Stories of My Greek Family*, that preserves many of the Gekas family recipes.

Iron Mask

From a 2004 interview with Doug and Rita Marvin.

Doug and Rita Marvin were known throughout Tucson for their gracious hospitality and delicious Continental fare long before they opened the Iron Mask in 1965. The Marvins had hosted diners at their own restaurant, Marow's on Grant Road. From there, they operated dining rooms at the Redwood Lounge, the Ghost Ranch Lodge and the Coat of Arms. Doug had even been chef/manager at the Davis-Monthan Air Force Base Officer's Club. But it was the Iron Mask that most people associate with the Marvins.

Doug was a young traveler from England when he met Rita. He was working in the kitchen at the Santa Rita Hotel, which included catering for the cast and crew of the movie *The Furies* in nearby Sonoita. He had some issues with his green card and had to be bonded. Rita just happened

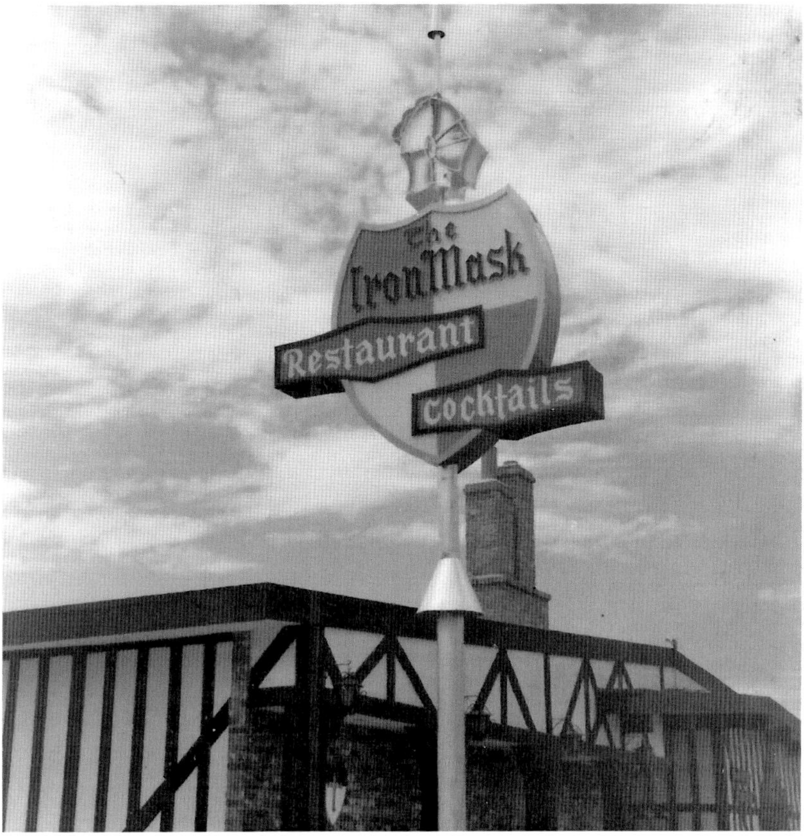

The Iron Mask sign could be seen for blocks on Tucson Boulevard. *The Marvin family.*

to be working at the bail bond office. It was love at first sight. They opened Marrow's in May 1952 and married in July of that year.[89]

The Iron Mask was opened in 1965, and for twenty-eight years, the Marvins served their special form of hospitality to diners in Tucson. The interior was like a dining room in an English inn. Trimmed in dark wood, the spacious dining room held a huge fireplace, royal crests and, of course, an iron mask. It held 110 seats. Leather booths lined the walls, with tables in the middle. The lighting was subdued, and if you were lucky enough to get a booth, dinner felt private in spite of all the activity in the rest of the room. Dinner was also served in the small, intimate bar.

The waitresses were dressed as serving wenches, and they would bring a chalkboard menu to every table and describe the evening's specials. Other items were listed on a handheld menu. In an online response to an article

I wrote in 2004 for the *Tucson Weekly*, one of the former "serving wenches" wrote with loving praise for her bosses. Her favorite dish was the cabrilla, and she admitted to bugging Doug for his trifle recipe, to no avail.[90]

Wines were mostly French or from California. All dinners came with the soup de jour or a choice of green salad or cottage cheese, potato or rice pilaf and a vegetable. The menu was classically Continental, and people loved it—snails Bourguignonne, turtle soup, stuffed mushrooms, chateaubriand, tenderloin of beef Oskar, curry of shrimp Bombay and more. Favorite desserts were Baked Alaska and a memorable peach Melba.[91]

Doug was a stickler for doing things right. He shopped daily to find the freshest vegetables and other items for dinner. He rendered the fat he used for French fries himself, carefully making sure that the fat was filtered to perfection. He was strict during service but a supportive boss once the kitchen closed.

Part of the charm of the Iron Mask was, of course, Rita. She ran the front of the house with grace and warmth. She knew everyone's name, what they liked to eat and drink and their favorite table. She treated all guests the

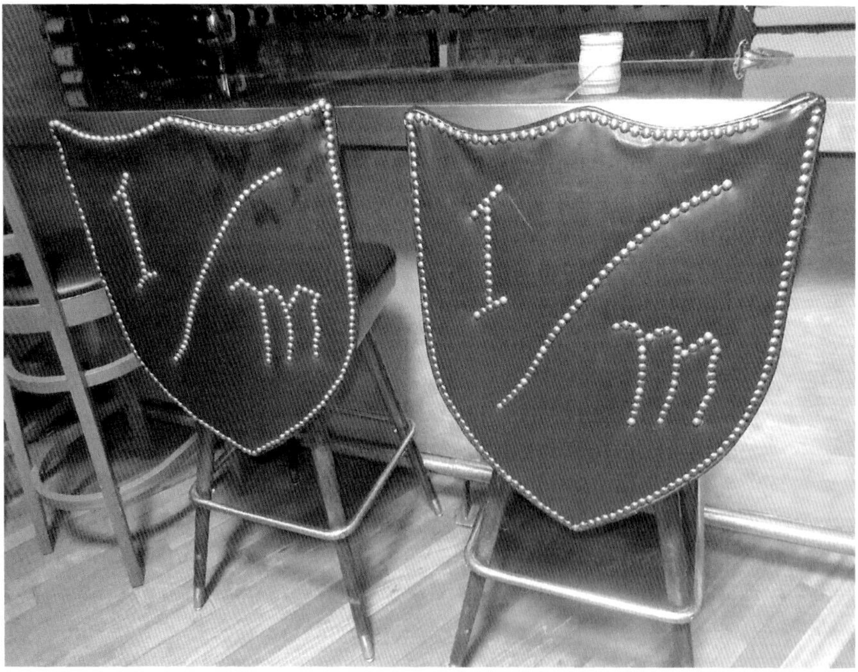

These chairs from the Iron Mask now sit at the bar at Kingfisher, the restaurant that moved in after the Iron Mask closed. *Author's collection.*

same, even Joe Bonanno, who ate there on a regular basis with his entourage. Other famous guests included Van Cliburn, John Wayne and Paul Newman.

The Iron Mask was where people went for special occasions. The private room, which held sixty people, was always hosting a birthday, an anniversary or a business dinner. Tucson, in the summer, can be painfully slow, even for a place as popular as the Iron Mask, so every July, the Marvins would close the restaurant and take their family on a vacation to Laguna Beach, California. They had two sons, Brian and Jeff, and one daughter, Karin.

Doug was a founding member of the American Culinary Foundation Chef's Association of Southern Arizona and was one of the first chefs elected to CASA's Hall of Fame in 1992. The Iron Mask and the Marvins received other numerous accolades over the years.

In 1993, an invitation was sent out to friends and family for the Farewell Dinner at the Iron Mask. Both Rita and Doug felt it was time to retire. Customers were saddened, but they understood. Rita died in September 2005 after a lengthy illness. The picture in her obituary showed Rita as most people remember her, elegantly dressed with a gracious smile on her face.

Doug remained active in the culinary community until his death in July 2015, just prior to the writing of this book. A memorial service was held at Kingfisher, which is the former site of the Iron Mask. Today, the cooler from the Iron Mask kitchen sits behind the bar there, and patrons can sit on the well-preserved stools that still grace the customer side of the bar. So, in a small way, the Iron Mask is still a part of Tucson.

Miracle Mile: Tucson's Historic Highway

This strip of roadway has played a major role in Tucson's hospitality history in more ways than one. Some of it was high style and other parts low life. But from the 1930s through the 2000s, Miracle Mile was the place to go for good eats.

At the convergence of Routes 80, 89 and 84, Miracle Mile was once one of the main ways in and out of town. In the 1930s, as motor traffic became the latest and greatest way to see America, the 1.5-mile stretch of concrete was renamed from Casa Grande Highway to Miracle Mile because it was such a model feat of engineering.[92]

Motor courts lined the street, and a few restaurants popped up. The site of a small barbecue stand that opened in 1929 was reopened in 1936 and named the Green Lantern. The building was easy to find because of the

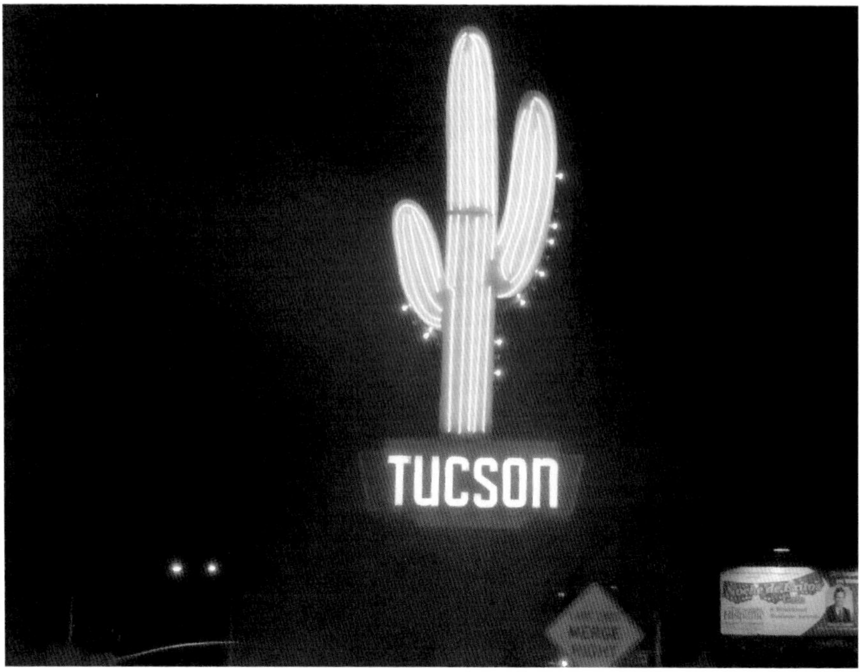

A neon saguaro announces the entry way to Miracle Mile. Other restored neon signs can be found just down the street. *Author's collection.*

huge neon lantern out front. At first, Randy Pool and his family lived on the property. They served everything from chicken and shrimp in baskets to T-bone steaks. Business was so successful that Pool was able expand and move the family to a house off site.[93]

In 1959, he sold the place to Dean Short, who changed the name to Ye Olde Lantern. Short had just sold his Panda Steak House. Short cranked up the concept and, of course, the prices.

Ye Olde Lantern was a little high end for that time, but nevertheless it had a big following. If there was a theme here, it might be called "English pub." The wood was black, and the booths were red vinyl. And the menu read like something out of *The Canterbury Tales*. "The Bill of Faer at Dinner" included categories such as "The Innkeeper Recommends," "The King's Own Beefe" and "Favourites of Henry VIII." It carried the English touch even in the descriptions of menu items. The Top Sirloin Yeoman Style, for example, was Friar Tuck's favorite, and the jumbo shrimp were fresh from the nets of the queen's fleet. The "reckoning" for dinner (meaning everything that came with dinner) included the

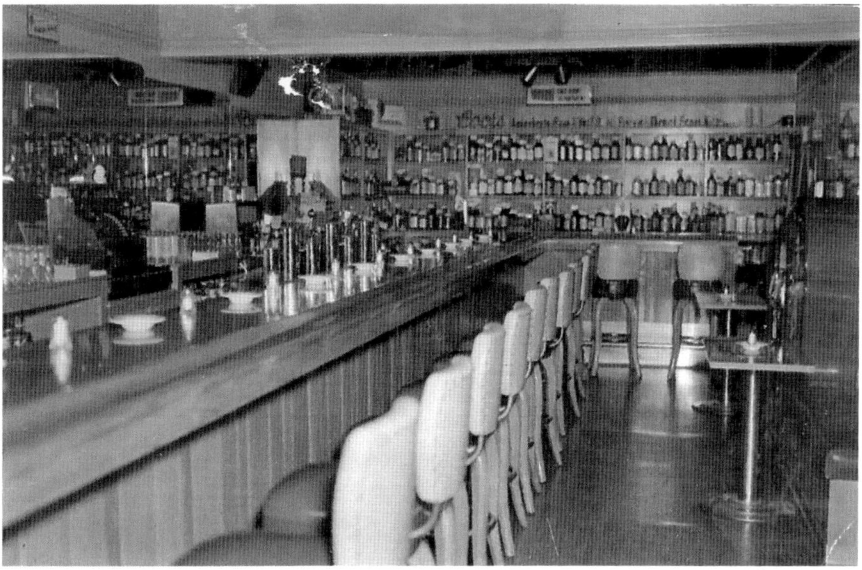

The Green Lantern. *From the collection of Dwight and Christy Schannep, American Antique Mall.*

"fabulous" relish tray, salad from the roving cart, a potato and bread. In spite of the flashy descriptions, the food here was delicious and well prepared. Regulars were loyal subjects.

In 1995, Short sold the place to Bob and Madeline Hawes. They changed very little about the place and ran it for eleven years until they retired in 2006. Parts of the building were torn down, and other parts were reconfigured. Today, it is the home of a local Elks Club. The sign is being restored as part of the Tucson Historic Preservation Foundation's Neon Tucson project, where the beautiful beacons of the past are restored to their former glowing glory.

Short owned several other restaurants on Miracle Mile. Ports O'Call was just up the street. Two other restaurants in town, El Corral and Kon Tiki, were also part of Short's stable. He wrote a weekly column for the *Tucson Citizen* called "Short's Shorts" in which he shared the happenings at each restaurant such as birthday celebrations, anniversaries and the like, complete with individual names. The Kon Tiki closed in early 2015; El Corral is still going strong but under new ownership.[94]

During the 1940s and 1950s, Ports O'Call was called the Pago Pago, which was extremely popular. The theme could be called "Island," complete with palm fringe and "Polynesian" servers serving "Polynesian" drinks. Live music featured Dude Vance and Louise Skeen, "Queen of the Keyboards."[95] At one time, live monkeys were kept in a glass cage in the cocktail lounge. The monkeys' behavior got them eighty-sixed quickly, and parrots took their place.

There were several owners prior to Short, but the dates are a little blurry. Homer Moore and Bob McAfee owned it together for a while, and Phil Kessler was also an owner, as was Jack Holcombe. A clip found on critiki.com also noted that Acheson Blakely was an owner. The clip mentioned that Acheson took care of the monkeys, so he must have been an early owner. A scene from *A Kiss Before Dying*, starring Robert Wagner as a murderous college student, was filmed there in 1956.

Short bought it in 1959 and renamed it Aku Aku. There was a fire in 1964, and thereafter the place was renamed Ports O'Call.[96] Other restaurants that lined the street include Gus & Andy's; the Northwoods, an A-frame building trimmed in snow; and two Mexican places: Club 21 and La Fuente.

In the late 1970s, in spite of having a "row" of successful restaurants, Miracle Mile developed a seedy reputation for prostitution and drug dealing. The city began a campaign to clear out the riffraff, with some success. But the motels suffered, as did some of the restaurants. Currently, there is a movement to revive the area that is meeting with great success. Motels are being turned into boutique motels. A few shops have sprung up on the far north side. The city, again, has begun to aggressively put a crunch on crime.

Oddly, though, there are only a few restaurants: Club 21, the lone holdout from the old days; Café Marcel, a tiny and relatively new crêperie; La Parilla Suiza, which serves Mexico City Mexican food and is located in the old Northwoods building; and Monterrey Court, a refurbished motor court known for its music.

The Scordatos

Technically speaking, Scordato's could be placed in the chapter about international cuisine since it served classic Italian dishes like osso buco and lasagna. But Scordato's was high end all the way, complete with soft white linen tablecloths and waiters dressed in tuxedos. Dining here was a special event.

People thought that James Scordato was crazy when he said he wanted to open a restaurant way out in the desert, but soon, thanks to quality food and warm hospitality, Scordato's became the go-to place for Tucsonans to spend an elegant evening or special occasion.

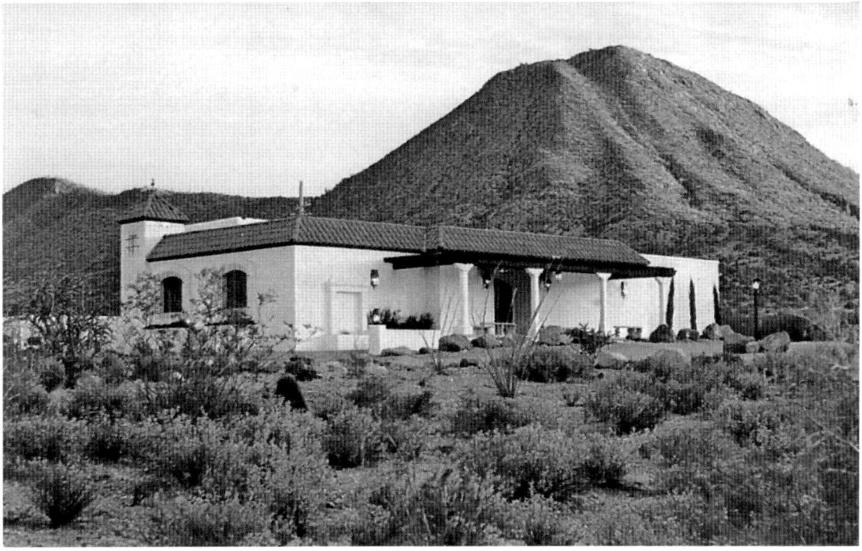

The long drive to Scordato's was always worth it. *From the collection of Dwight and Christy Schannep, American Antique Mall.*

James Scordato came from a restaurant family in New Jersey, but he'd always wanted to be a cowboy. So he moved his wife, Ann, and four children to the tiny town of Duncan, Arizona, where he became the marshal of the county.[97] But food service was in his blood, and eventually Jim moved everyone to Tucson and purchased the Tucson Rolling Snack Bar. But even that wasn't quite enough for Jim, so he bought property west of town because he couldn't find the kind of food he'd grown up eating.

Each member of the family owned a share in the restaurant, even teenager Danny.[98] Opening in 1972, Scordato's offered only the best. It was the first restaurant that butchered its own veal. In a town where people thought veal Parmigiana meant ground-up meat in a bland red sauce, Scordato's served veal loin in an authentic fashion.[99] The recipes were from Ann's family in Italy and featured the best ingredients available. The kitchen had state-of-the-art equipment.

The wine list was well over three hundred bottles strong, something unheard of at the time. Waiters served the house Caesar salad tableside. When opera wasn't playing overhead, classically trained sister Patricia was at the piano. Brothers Jim Jr. and Joe helped their dad in the kitchen, while little brother Danny ran the front of the house like a longtime professional, even though he was barely out of his teens. It was a true family affair. Guests included movies stars, politicians and the likes of Joe Bonanno, who was a regular. One customer made special trips to Tucson just to eat there.

In 1980, James Sr. sold his share of the restaurant to his four children. But as good a team as they were in the beginning, things began to fall apart. Danny sold his share and opened Daniel's in Palomino Plaza, completely on the other side of town. Then Jim, Joe Jr. and Patricia opened Scordato's on Broadway, which didn't last very long. Joe then opened Joe Scordato's Trattoria Giuseppe on Tanque Verde Road.[100] That left Jim and his wife as sole owners of the family legacy. He sold the place to Evangelos Vassious, who continued to use the Scordato name.

Vassious eventually sued Joe over the use of the family name, claiming that he lost business. Vassious won. Trattoria Giuseppe closed, and the family was barred from using their own name.[101]

Daniel's was the only true Scordato restaurant left, and although it was immensely popular, Danny will admit that perhaps he had bitten off more than he could chew. He filed for bankruptcy and took on a partner, Richard Katz. A move to Saint Philip's Plaza didn't help, and he bowed out in 1992.[102]

Daniel's, Part II

People welcomed the change in ownership, and Daniel's continued to be a place where people could enjoy a relaxing evening in an elegant atmosphere. Dinner started with a complimentary flamed goat cheese with tomato sauce and bread for dipping. Guests loved it. Caesar salads were made tableside. The veal chop was one of the most popular items on the menu. And the wine list was comparable to those found in bigger cities. Daniel's won the local Silver Spoon Award four years in a row.[103] But then Daniel's closed in 2000 without notice or explanation.

Charles

Charles was one of the last great formal restaurants in Tucson. Charles Kerr was a brilliant restaurateur who had held the post of maître d' at The Tack Room when it earned its five-star rating. When he opened his own place on the grounds of the former El Dorado Country Club, he brought legions of fans with him. The restaurant was located at the end of a long, brick, Italian Cyprus–lined drive. Valet service was provided, so there was no worry of where to park or a long walk in high heels.

The previous occupant had been the Palm Court Restaurant, but Kerr completely revamped the entire space. The floors were slate and the ceilings beamed wood. Several fireplaces added a warm glow. The dining area was divided into several rooms: two large dining rooms, with huge picture windows that allowed for amazing views of the Catalina and Rincon Mountain Ranges and the exquisitely manicured grounds; the Bethaney Court, a bar with seating for dining; and the Oak Room, with curtained booths for a more private meal. Arches divided the spaces, with each arch embossed with a large letter *C* on them. On most evenings, music was provided by a concert pianist on the grand piano.[104]

Men were required to wear jackets, which would be provided by the house from the collection in a closet should someone show up coatless. Food was no less spectacular. Tableside service by well-dressed male servers included steak tartare, Caesar salad and flambéed rack of lamb, among other items.

In the kitchen, whole sides of veal were broken down and every bit used in chops, osso buco, sauces and soups. Specialties were exclusive to Charles and had such elegant names as Lobster Macao, Roast Duckling Waldorf, Veal Charles and Veal Dorado. All breads and baked goods were made in house.[105] Indeed, dining at Charles was an elegant and memorable experience.

After Charles closed, the space was reopened as Stone Ashley, an elegant spot with tiny special touches, such as having specific chairs for women's purses, but nothing came close to what Charles Kerr served up at Charles.

The Game Changers

Janos

From an interview with Janos Wilder, July 2015.

On Halloween 1983, Janos Wilder opened his eponymous restaurant in the heart of historic Tucson. Janos, the restaurant, was located in the Hiram Stevens House, which was part of the Tucson Museum of Art and Historic Block. The space was elegant and authentic, with lovely touches.

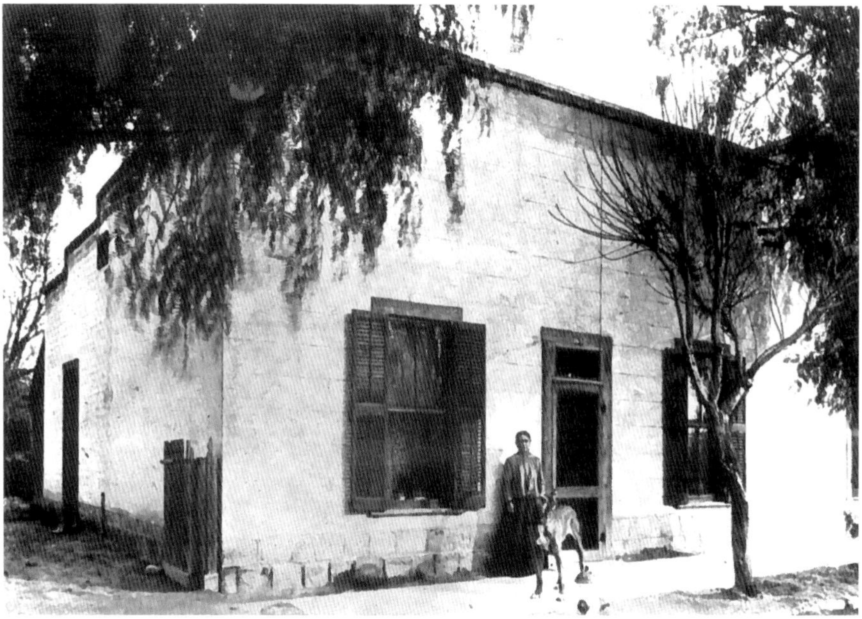

Petra Stevens and dog in front of Stevens House, circa 1890. *Gift of the Velasco family, from the collection of the Tucson Museum of Art and Historic Block.*

Wilder and his wife, Rebecca, enlisted the help of their friend Rory McCarthy, who along with Rebecca turned the nicely preserved home into a warm, welcoming space complete with local art and specially designed furniture, much of which he built himself. Riffing on antiques from Mexico, the furniture fit perfectly in the historic space.

The food was decidedly different from what most Tucsonans were used to. In fact, on that first night, one man sent his lobster dish back because it wasn't served in its shell and had a carrot and spinach mousse on the plate instead of drawn butter. In his cookbook, *Janos: Recipes and Tales from a Southwest Restaurant*, the chef described the dish as "a metaphor of my entire cooking philosophy."[106]

Fortunately, that man was the exception, as Janos was a hit from that first night. People were drawn to this new style of cooking. They had never seen or tasted their familiar southwestern ingredients prepared in such a way. Janos was taking his training in French cooking and creating dishes using local ingredients such tepary beans, prickly pear cactus, desert honey, chiles and such. He turned them into spectacular dishes with a modern yet classic style. "We were on a steep learning curve," said Wilder, "and we got busy fast. It was exciting, fun, innovating, and there were no limits. We saw no limits to how good we could be or what we could do."

New ground was broken almost daily because the menus changed daily, something almost unheard of at a time when Continental dining reigned supreme. "I'd get up and see what was available, what was in the market. I'd bring in things we'd never worked with at the time," said Wilder.

But it wasn't just the food. Janos and his team, which included Ellen Burke Van Slyke and Elizabeth Woolls, were turning the old male-dominated front-of-the-house system on its head as well. Janos just wanted to get the best people and streamline the service so that "your server would have a one-on-one relationship with your guest." And people noticed, not just in Tucson but in the rest of the country as well. The *New York Times* had a small write-up. The local press had a playful article about where the city councilmen were spending their money—namely at Janos. And while the tone from the paper was a bit of an admonishment, it was wonderful for business.

In a 1984 review by Tom and Laurie Pew in the *Tucson Citizen*, words like "heavenly" and "superb" and "marvelous" were used to describe one dish after another. The décor got thumbs up, as did the service.[107] The positive reviews continued year after year because the team at Janos was always passionate about making people happy.

One of the biggest things that Janos took away from his time in France beyond techniques was that "at the heart of French cooking was the relationship between the chef and the garden." And to that extent, he had advertised for gardeners before he advertised for staff. He knew that if he wanted to cook French food, he would have to utilize the nearby ingredients. "The things I put on the menu weren't the things people were used to seeing. They'd never seen the dishes that were on my menu before because they never existed until that morning in many cases."

And even though the menu varied daily, certain dishes became local favorites. Wilder had a way with chiles rellenos, stuffed fresh chiles. But instead of the bland cheddar cheese found everywhere in town, Wilder stuffed his with lobster and brie, truffled wild mushrooms, Roquefort, apples, mangos and a whole assortment of unexpected ingredients. Chiles were even used in desserts.

In spite of the popularity of Janos, the board at the Tucson Museum of Art wanted to do something different with the space. The city council went to bat for the restaurant, but things just didn't work out. So, with plenty of lead time, the Wilders started to look for a different space. Downtown was always an option, but seeing the competition heading toward the foothills, the Wilders opted for the grounds of the Westin La Paloma Resort. The Westin had a standalone building it wanted to fill, and so Janos became a foothills restaurant. As different as that space was from the Stevens House, it also had beautiful views of the city and a lot more room. Thus J Bar was born.

Janos, due to its price point, was still a little "elitist," and J Bar allowed Wilder to step back from that a bit. The room was a splash of colors not found at its more sedate sister next door. The food was also a lot more fun. One favorite was the J Dawg, Wilder's take on a local favorite called the Sonoran hot dog. In the original, a hot dog is grilled and then wrapped in bacon and topped with cowboy beans, cheddar cheese, tomatoes, chiles, grilled onions and mayonnaise. Served on a specially made soft bun, they're killer good, but Wilder, in his inimitable way, kicked it up several notches. Chorizo replaced the bacon, black beans were used instead of the cowboy beans, the mustard was whole grain, the onions were red and then there were pickled nopalitos (prickly pear cactus).

But then the Westin went into bankruptcy, and new owners didn't get what Janos/J Bar was all about. So, in 2012, Wilder closed both spaces. An era ended, but as is typical with Wilder's style, it ended on a good note, under his terms, not owing anyone anything. Today, Wilder works his magic back where he started, in downtown Tucson. The restaurant, Downtown Kitchen and Cocktails, isn't Janos, but it remains a great place for great food.

Café Terra Cotta

From an interview with Donna Nordin and Don Luria, July 2015.

"In order to keep me here," said Chef Donna Nordin, "what he did was say, 'Why don't we open a restaurant?'" The "he" of which she speaks is her husband, Don Luria, and the restaurant they opened was Café Terra Cotta. By the time Nordin came to Tucson to teach cooking classes, she had established herself as a nationally recognized chef and teacher. Don, along with Candace Grogan, owned and operated the Tasting Kitchen Cooking School and Gourmet to Go catering company.

So, Nordin took Luria up on the offer and, together with Grogan, formed a partnership. It took a few years to get funding and find the perfect spot, but within weeks of Café Terra Cotta's opening, the place was jumping. This was in 1986, and up until then, there had been nothing like what Café Terra Cotta was doing. They called it Contemporary

Southwestern, and in a city that knew its chiles and beans, Café Terra Cotta showed locals a new way of eating.

The restaurant was located at the relatively new Saint Philip's Plaza, at the base of the Santa Catalina foothills, Tucson's fast-growing upscale neighborhood. It was an ideal spot. People had the expendable income, and Café Terra Cotta was just down the road. They decked out the open space in the colors of the desert and hung artwork from Arizona and New Mexico artists. Later, some of the artwork was used for labels for Café Terra Cotta's private wine label.

While the Contemporary Southwestern concept was solid, finding the perfect name took a little longer. Then, on an "eating project" trip to San Francisco, Nordin noticed a faceplate made of terra cotta on a table at a restaurant and thought, "Terra cotta…now that sounds southwestern!" They added the "Café" part because they wanted the place to be casual.

Nordin believes that the restaurant's sudden popularity had something to do with the fact that a few weeks after opening, she got a call to be part of *Great Chefs of the West* series on PBS. Then Mimi Sheraton wrote about Café Terra Cotta as well, garnering even more national recognition. From the local perspective, they received a glowing review from Laurie and Tom Pew, the best-known restaurant reviewers in Tucson at that time. The Pews were getting set to retire and told Nordin and Luria that they'd try the place; if they didn't like it, they wouldn't write a review. The restaurant had only been open a few weeks, hardly enough time to give a fair review. But the Pews loved just about everything about the place and wrote a great review, and the crowds followed in droves.

Nordin and Luria brought in Kevin Baker, a friend of Donna's from California who had made a name for himself opening restaurants. Baker was a great chef with a temper to match but was the ideal fit. "We were one of the first places to have a wood-burning pizza oven," said Luria. Baker spent nights scouting pizza joints around town. He found a young pizza maker named Doug Levy at a tiny local place. "I had never worked in a kitchen like that before," said Levy, referring to Baker's style. But Levy loved it there, eventually working his way up through the kitchen.[108] Today, Levy has his own successful restaurant, Feast, in Tucson.

Another early hire was Jeff Azersky, now of Kingfisher. Azersky had recently moved to Tucson from Boston. He stepped in when Baker left and laughed when he spoke about getting hired. "They [Nordin and Grogan] said, 'Good, you know what arugula is,'" he said.[109] Azersky eventually helped open Prima Donna, Nordin and Luria's short-lived Italian restaurant, and then moved on to Boccata before opening Kingfisher. The owners also

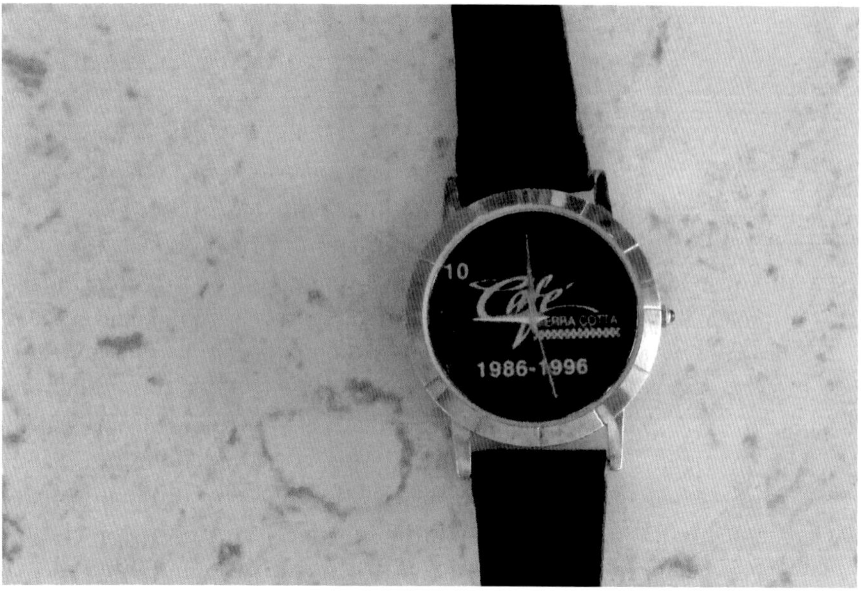

The watch celebrates ten years of great hospitality at Café Terra Cotta. *Author's collection; watch courtesy of Rocco DiGrazia.*

had Los Mayas, a "very regional and authentic" Mexican place. All three restaurants were in Saint Philip's.

When Azersky left as executive chef, Marianne Baines took over. Baines had worked in several kitchens in Tucson and had just returned from a stint in San Francisco. Working at Café Terra Cotta turned out to be just what she was looking for. Her sous chef, Steven Critcher, taught her about moles, chiles and Southwest flavors, and because Nordin gave her staff the leeway to be creative, Baines loved her time at Terra Cotta, which seems to be the general consensus of most of the people who worked in the kitchen.[110] Charlene Badman, a Scottsdale-based James Beard nominee, also worked her way up through the Terra Cotta kitchens.

Café Terra Cotta was also groundbreaking in other ways, one being the use of local ingredients, which led to another innovation, a seasonal menu. Still, due to demand from diners, certain dishes were perennially on the menu. "We could never leave off the shrimp stuffed with goat cheese. We could never leave off the tortilla soup. We could never leave off the chocolate mousse pie," said Nordin. Other signature plates that hung on included the crème brûlée, the garlic custard and various pizzas. The stuffed poblanos were also always on the menu, but Nordin noted that this dish got tweaked now and then.

Around 1989, the recession hit Tucson hard; the plaza went into receivership, and the owners sold everything. Somewhere around this time, Grogan left to pursue other interests. This change in ownership of the plaza made it difficult for Nordin and Luria. They had a fifteen-year lease that was renewable every five years. Rent had been reasonable, but the new owners of the plaza had done their research and upped the rent to $33,000 per month, making the profit margin in the minus column. For that amount, Luria said they could build a new building.

In order to save Terra Cotta, Nordin and Luria filed for Chapter 13 and closed Los Mayas and Prima Donna. (For a short while, there was a Café Terra Cotta in Scottsdale.) It was time for a move. After fifteen years at Saint Philip's Plaza, Café Terra Cotta moved to a freestanding building several miles northeast of the original site. The "Café" part was dropped, but little else changed, except for the fact that they now owned the building. Also, Luria's son, Michael, and his wife, Maya, were active in the business.

The reputation grew. Famous people made a point of eating there. When Paul Newman, Joanne Woodward and their daughter arrived in town to spend time at the chic Canyon Ranch Spa, they drove directly

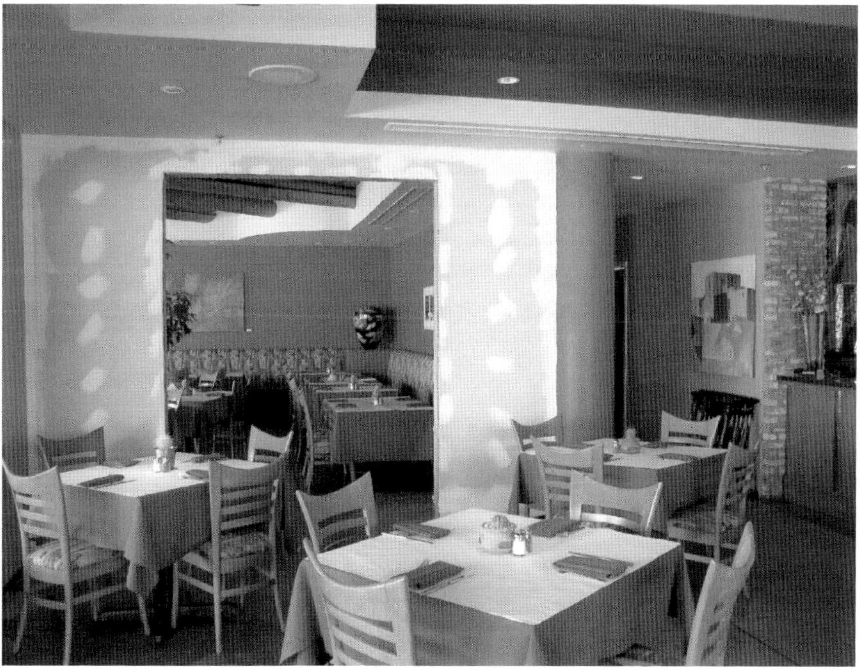

Terra Cotta interior. *Dr. Patricia Sparks.*

Terra Cotta's Signature Shrimp Stuffed with Goat Cheese

Serves 4

1 pound large shrimp (16 to 20 per pound), butterflied
4 ounces goat cheese
4 ounces cream cheese
1 medium garlic clove, minced
1 tablespoon cream
4 tablespoons chopped cilantro
salt and pepper to taste
2 tablespoons olive oil
4 medium tomatoes, peeled, seeded and chopped
1 tablespoon chopped jalapeño chile
juice of 1 lime

1. Preheat oven to 350 degrees F. Bake the shrimp until barely firm, about 2 minutes. Remove and cool slightly.
2. Mix the goat cheese, cream cheese, garlic, cream and half the cilantro together and season with salt and pepper. Pipe the cheese mixture onto the butterflied shrimp with a pastry bag or spread it on thickly with a knife.
3. Turn up the oven to 400 degrees F and return the stuffed shrimp to bake for about 3 more minutes, or until the shrimp is opaque. Meanwhile, heat the oil in a skillet and cook the tomatoes, covered, until they exude their juice, about 5 minutes. Add the remaining cilantro, jalapeño, salt, pepper and lime juice to taste. Cook uncovered until the moisture is almost evaporated, leaving just enough for a runny texture.
4. Spoon the tomato coulis on a plate and serve the stuffed shrimp on top.

Note: To butterfly shrimp, remove all but the last section of the shell. Cut deeply along the outside, cutting almost but not all the way through. Remove the vein on the outer edge. When the shrimp cook, the tail will curl up.

Variation: These shrimp may also be served at room temperature as an hors d'oeuvre.

From *Contemporary Southwest: The Café Terra Cotta Cookbook* (1999).

from the airport to Terra Cotta. Nordin and Luria gave them a bottle of Arizona wine, a Sonoita cabernet, which the Newmans took with them to the resort.

Luria had met Muhammad Ali on a flight out of Cincinnati years earlier and told him that if he were ever in Tucson to come and have dinner. He did, bringing his wife, daughter and young son. Ali was already showing signs of Parkinson's disease and had made a bit of a mess under the table. When his family went shopping up the road, Ali began to clean up after himself. Nordin and Luria rushed in and took care of things, asking Ali if he needed anything. All Ali wanted was to have his picture taken with the pretty girls at the front desk.

On the morning of July 5, 2004, the call came in that there was a fire at Terra Cotta. Although it was never really determined what caused the fire, it took five months to clean up the damage. Michael took over a lot of the work, as Don was busy overseeing the Tucson Originals and its offshoots in other cities, the Tucson Culinary Festival and other interests. Donna was helping her parents transition into assisted living.

A decision was made to close Terre Cotta in 2007. There were no regrets. "We made an impact on the cuisine and the community," said Nordin. "We kind of put Tucson on the map." Fortunately for her fans, Nordin's cookbook, *Contemporary Southwest: The Café Terra Cotta Cookbook*, can still be found online.

Fuego

Long before he opened Fuego in January 1996, Chef Alan Zeman was making a name for himself as an advocate for southwestern cuisine. When he was featured in the May 1987 issue of *Bon Appétit* magazine, Zeman raved about the flavors of the area.

He worked at resorts and country clubs in Tucson and a few restaurants as well. He was a part of the *Great Chefs of the West* series on public TV. He graduated from the Culinary Institute of America. He created a company that sold his spice blends and prickly pear sauces.[111] But then he opened Fuego and, to quote another famous chef, "kicked it up a notch"—or two or three. "I didn't want to do fine dining like The Tack Room," he said. "I didn't want to be Chili's. I wanted to be in between." And in spite of the fact that the restaurant's price range leaned more toward the high end, Zeman succeeded in his goal.[112]

The dining room was dressed in dark wood and low lighting; it was intimate and romantic. "We tried to do eclectic things. We focused on service. We focused on wine…just to have quality and have it presented right," he said. This meant fresh and seasonal before those ideas became popular. There was a basic menu, but in keeping with the fresh theme, they typed up a new menu every day. Seafood, game and wine were a big part of the picture. A popular feature was Mussel Madness on Mondays, when diners could enjoy a few mussels on the house during happy hour. Oysters were big and were served on the half shell and in entrées.

Fuego was one of the first places to serve ostrich, although Zeman pointed out that the big bird came on the menu almost by accident. It was the time of the "mad cow" scare, and magazines were featuring ostrich as a tasty alternative. The fact that there was a nearby ostrich ranch helped, and soon it was on the menu every night in some way, either as an appetizer or an entrée. It was often served with Zeman's signature polenta. "We treated it like veal scallopini," said Zeman.[113]

True to its name, Fuego was all about fire. Many dishes were flambéed at the table. A southwestern-influenced flaming seafood dish included shrimp, scallops, chorizo, onions, peppers and garlic flamed with tequila. Another dish, the smoking lamb shank, comprised lamb with roasted garlic and roasted red chiles; then, at the table, a sprig of rosemary was lit. Even desserts like the bananas foster were lit. Perhaps the most memorable dish, although it wasn't set aflame, was the prickly pear pork, pork loin that was slathered with Zeman's own prickly pear sauce.

The kitchen made just about everything from scratch: sauces, sausages, pâtés, charcuterie and breads, right on down to the hamburger buns. The smoked salmon on the menu was smoked in house. The kitchen staff was a mix of top-caliber chefs and young talent, such as Karen "Spike" Ames, who became a first-class pastry chef. Another young chef, Ryan Clark, is today one of the top chefs in Tucson and has his own successful restaurant, Agustin Kitchen. Zeman taught Clark not just technique but also how a good restaurant is run. Clark considers Zeman his mentor to this day: "You came into work every day, and you knew how it was going to be. At four o'clock, Alan would be at the lead station, and he'd break down all the proteins. He would be on the line at 5:00 p.m. plating all the dishes. That's why he was so successful, because he was always there"[114]

Clark learned a lot working for Zeman, but he also noted that Zeman has a wild sense of humor. Everyone enjoyed the work. Zeman also hosted a radio program called *The Dinner Hour* for eleven years during which he and a co-host interviewed chefs and food industry people.

In 2007, Zeman announced that he was closing Fuego. It was time, and the dining scene in Tucson was changing. Today, he still sells his Southwest

Original products and works for a company called Rational, which produces high-end professional kitchen appliances. When asked if he misses the kitchen life, Zeman answered with his signature wit: "Oh, for about ten minutes." Then he added, "It's the people I miss."[115] The people miss Alan Zeman, too.

New but Not Nouvelle

Boccata

One can hardly talk about the lost restaurants of Tucson without mentioning Ellen Burke Van Slyke. Described as "Miss Personality Plus Times Ten," Van Slyke helped change the way Tucsonans dined. Her first restaurant job in Tucson was at Janos, where she ran the front of the house. She helped move forward the idea that fine dining need not be pretentious and formal.

In 1989, she along with her husband and her brother, Matt, opened Boccata Bistro Bar on the corner of River and Craycroft Roads. Boccata, as it became known, was just what the neighborhood needed. There, after a long, hard day at the office, one could enjoy a nosh and a glass of wine or beer in a warm, welcoming space where literally "everyone knew your name."[116] The food was Southern French/Northern Italian (in Italian, the word *boccata* means either a mouthful or a breath of fresh air), and the bar played a big part of the experience. Regulars popped in once or twice a week. Some had their own table, their favorite server and their own signature meal. Van Slyke estimated that 85 percent of customers were regulars.[117]

Boccata was one of the first places to feature mussels as a specialty. Steamed in white wine and garlic butter, the happy hour special that was served with a glass of wine or a Bass ale brought in the crowds. Profiteroles were the way to end a meal. Another signature dish was the Penne Ciao Bella: penne pasta, grilled chicken, artichoke hearts, roasted red peppers and pine nuts in a light gorgonzola cream sauce. Van Slyke noted that even now people tell her how much they miss the dish.[118]

Summer in Tucson can be slow for just about any business, so restaurants are known to have special deals and events to bring in customers. One summer, the team decided to celebrate Bastille Day, July 14. It was such a hit that the next year it became Bastille Week and then, for years to follow, Bastille Month. In August, Italy got a nod with the Palio Festival.

It's All in the Family

From an interview with Matt Burke, July 2015.

Say the name Burke to anybody in the hospitality business in Tucson, and they're likely to ask, "Which one?" That's because, in addition to Ellen, there's John, Matt and Brian; at one time or another, they owned some of the most popular restaurants in the 1980s and early 1990s. Matt owned Barrio, a brasserie, on Sixth Street downtown. Brother John opened Kingfisher with Jim Murphy, Jeff Azersky and Tim Ivankovich. He left there and bought Fiorito's with wife Tess O'Shea.

Boccata closed its doors in 1997. Van Slyke also had a smaller version of Boccata called Pronto. Located on Speedway Boulevard just east of the University of Arizona, Pronto was a place to grab a quick meal that was flavorful and healthy. Well ahead of its time with a fast-casual approach to service, Pronto offered great pastas, salads and sandwiches. Desserts from an in-house bakery were popular as well. Pronto was open from 1991 to 1999.

Van Slyke went on to open the Ventana Room at Loew's Ventana Canyon Resort. Today, she works for Hilton International but still has fond memories of her time in Tucson, just as many Tucsonans have fond memories of Ellen Van Slyke.

The Solarium

When people recall the Solarium, the talk is about the structure as much as the food. It opened in 1974 and added a whole new vibe to the culinary—and architectural—scene. Set in a small patch of tall, shady trees, the Solarium was three stories of wood and glass. It was rustic and modern at the same time. The large, heavy front door was a work of art, more sculpture than entryway.

Inside, the split layers contained two bars, one on the ground floor and one upstairs; plenty of hanging plants; booths molded from cement; angles that allowed for intimacy; and lots of glittering glass. From the first floor, diners could see all the way up to the third floor because the ceilings rose so high. There was a sense of space, a swirling airiness; some called it "coastal Californian."

The Solarium featured a hip menu, as well. Crab legs were popular, and the prime rib rivaled any found at nearby steakhouses. Chef Jonathan Landeen, who worked at the Solarium in its heyday, noted that the Monte Cristo sandwich was probably "the best I've ever had." Two soups were always on the menu, and desserts brought raves from local reviewers.[119] On weekends, there was always live entertainment.

In spite of the cool, hip vibe, the crowds were a mixed lot. It was the kind of place you could bring your parents—the kind of place they would remember. In 1999, a fire reduced the Solarium to ashes. It was later found to be arson.

Jerome's

Jerome's food could best be described as Cajun-Southwest. With one of the first mesquite grills in Tucson (Chef Marianne Baines, now pastry chef at Kingfisher, remembered lugging logs of the heavy wood to the fire), blackened fish took on a smokier flavor. Jerome's was the brainchild of Jerome Soldevere, who was a creative chef with a story to tell.

Jerome Soldevere opened Jerome's in 1983 and brought fusion food to Tucson. The décor may have been French country, but the vibe was certainly different. So was the food. "It was something Tucson did not have. They had Mexican. They had seafood," said Jim Murphy, executive chef and owner of Kingfisher.[120] Murphy and Baines talked about breaking down whole rear sides of veal. Fish were brought in whole, mostly from Mexico. Rabbits, frogs…everything was whole. Red fish, something not seen at too many other places, was on the menu. There was even an in-house bakery that made all the breads and a killer Arizona pecan chocolate rum pie.

As befitting any Cajun kitchen, fish and seafood ruled. The barbecue in-the-shell shrimp was served in a garlicky lemon sauce. The raw bar served clams, oysters, calamari, ceviche and shrimp cocktail. Meat lovers didn't lack for anything with the blackened prime rib and veal Tanque Verde, which combined veal, shrimp, spinach and green chiles topped with an herbed hollandaise.[121] "It was fun," said Murphy. Customers felt the same way.

Soon, blackened anything could be found on menus all over town, but Jerome's will always be remembered as innovative and groundbreaking. It closed in 1995.

Nonie

Before Nonie came along, the A-frame structure on Grant Road just east of Tucson Boulevard had been home to many different and short-lived restaurants. Early on it had been a Bavarian restaurant, and then it became the restaurant for a local ashram, complete with your choice of macrobiotic meals. There was a pizza place in there somewhere, as well as a few places that were open for such a short time that their names are forgotten.

Then Christopher Leonard came along and everything changed, including Tucson's knowledge of Creole and Cajun foods. Until that time, those two

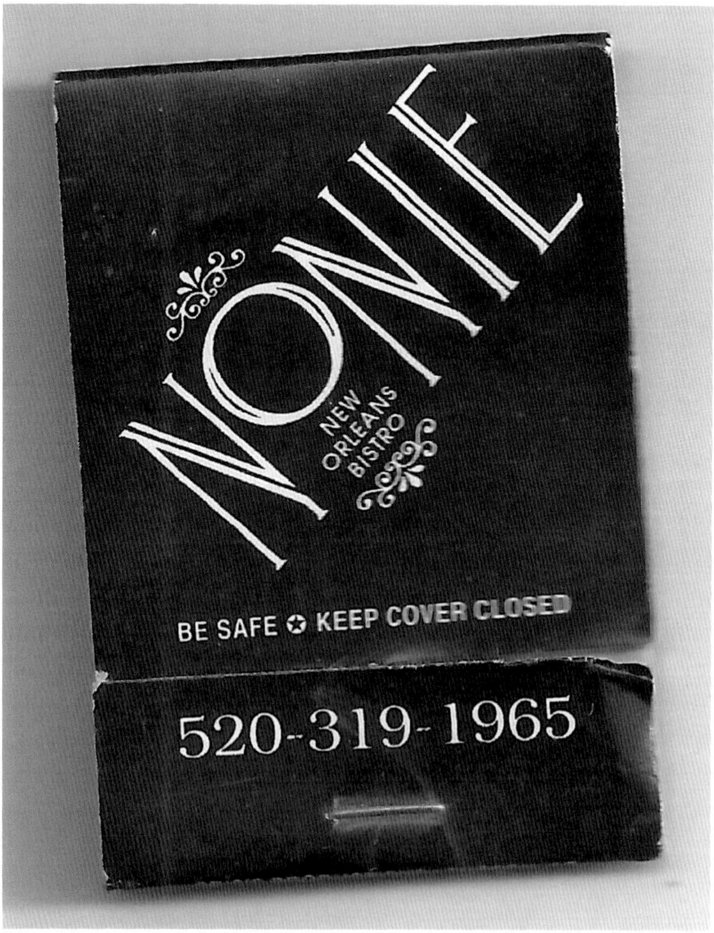

Nonie meant Cajun, Creole and bon temps. *From the collection of Rebecca Cowan.*

cuisines were interchanged, and if there were any restaurants of either kind in town, they were probably "theme" restaurants with all sorts of gimmicks. But there was nothing gimmicky about Nonie; it was the real thing. Gumbo, jambalaya, crawfish, blackened meats and red beans and rice were all on the menu. So were fine cocktails and a *laissez les bon temps rouler* attitude. In 1998, Nonie was the Reader's Choice for "Best New Restaurant" in the *Tucson Weekly*'s yearly Best of Tucson poll. (Nonie opened in 1997, but the voting covered the previous year.)[122]

Leonard's inspiration was his own nonie: his grandmother Florentine Rive. Many of the dishes were her recipes. Appetizers included fried pickles, alligator tail and oysters on the half shell. The gumbo and jambalaya changed daily. The pasta dishes won high praise, especially the house Nonie fettuccini, where shrimp, scallops and artichokes came together in a creamy tomato sauce that packed some heat. The crawfish etouffee was also a winner. Every year, when crawfish were in season, Nonie would serve the tiny crustaceans in huge mounds in an all-you-can-eat manner.[123]

Leonard closed Nonie to pursue other interests. A few other Cajun/Creole restaurants opened in Tucson, but none ever came close to the food, ambiance or success that was Nonie.

Sam Fox: Native Son

These days, Sam Fox runs an empire of restaurants all over the county, but Tucson is proud to call him a native son. He grew up working in his parents' restaurant, the Hungry Fox, and opened his own first restaurant, Gilligan's, sometime in the late 1980s.

Gilligan's was situated in Plaza Antigua, a tiny little shopping area that sat along the Rillito River at Campbell Avenue. It was a perfect meeting place. Families could find reasonably priced meals and spend time on the lovely patio. Co-workers could meet after a long day for a few brews or a cocktail and a snack. The young and the hip could mingle to their hearts' content later in the evening. The food was casually American—nothing to write home about but consistent and well prepared.

Gilligan's closed rather abruptly, but Fox went on to open Wildflower (which is still open) and Bistro Zin. Bistro Zin was a game changer in many ways, especially when it came to wine. The wine program was more modern and worldly than what was going on in the rest of the city. Here customers could enjoy a wide variety of wine flights, something unheard of in Tucson at the time, according to *Tucson Cooks!* The wine list was big for not being a Continental place, and many of the wines were from smaller wineries, thanks to Regan Jasper, who was the wine master for the company.

Dark, sexy, romantic, Zin was "adult," according to Ralph Avella, who worked there. It would've easily fit in a bigger city like Chicago or New York. The menu was American with French influences. Foie gras was one of the most popular items on the menu. Avella said that on an average evening, twenty orders of the house foie gras were served. People raved about the seafood options. The duck came with a plum wine reduction sauce that Avella said was unmatched. And desserts, thanks to Karen "Spike" Adams, were over the top. Her Bars of Zin were a tribute to chocolate in all its forms.

Bistro Zin closed in 2007 to make room for another Fox Concept Restaurant, ZinBurger. Bars of Zin can be found there, but only in a shake.

Anthony's in the Catalinas

The one restaurant that industry people suggested to be included in this book is Anthony's in the Catalinas. Anthony Martino had worked in the finest restaurants in the city for decades. His reputation was impeccable. So, when he decided to open his own place in 1989, people were excited. Martino took everything he knew about dining and service and created an icon.

He choose a prime location on the northeast corner of Campbell Avenue and Sunrise Road. Formerly the site of Los Campanas de Catalinas, the dining room offered stunning views of the Catalina Mountains on one side and the city on the other. Dinner at sunset was a show of light and shadow and stunning desert colors. Then, as the lights rose on the city, diners felt as though they were floating on an enchanted dark sea with sparkling diamonds all around.

The servers hovered just enough to meet every need, usually before being asked. The food was Continental fare prepared with the finest ingredients. Appetizers included duck mousse and black truffle terrine and escargot de

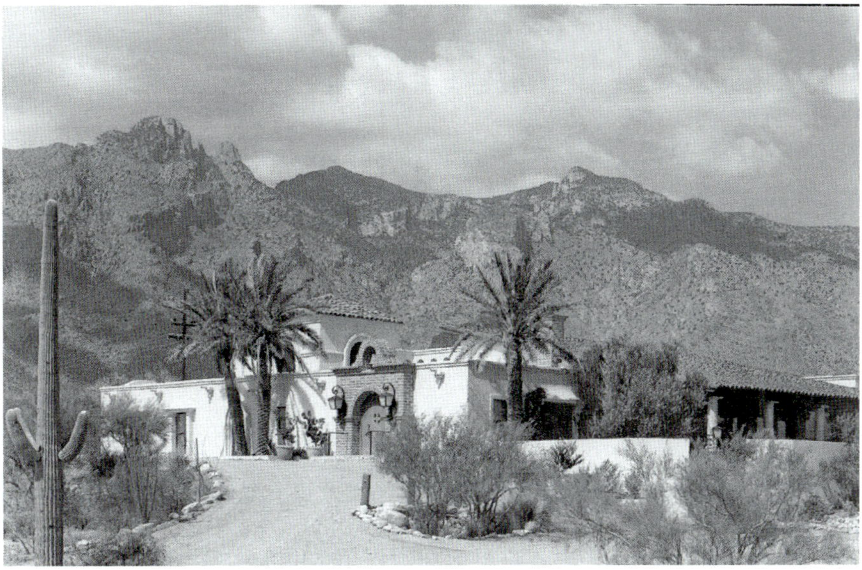

With some of the best views of the city, Anthony's in the Catalinas was a magical place. *Author's collection.*

chef. Entrées ranged from a pistachio pork chop to marinated trio of quail. Desserts could be accompanied by a fine cigar from the house's humidor.[124] But it was the wine list that distinguished Anthony's from all the other fine dining restaurants in the city: 1,700 bottles ranging in price from $25 to a rarefied $15,000. Anthony's first won the Wine Spectator Grand Award in 1983 and every year afterward, and it was on the list for one of seventy-six top restaurants in the world for wine.[125]

Numerous culinary awards, both local and national, were a regular occurrence. But like many places, 2008 was a bad year for restaurants, and fine dining/high-end places were hit especially hard. Business slowed, and then, in 2011, Martino's wife, Brooke, pleaded guilty to tax evasion. Anthony's closed shortly thereafter.[126]

Chapter 5

From Around the World to the Old Pueblo

Immigrants who come to America often find that opening a restaurant is a great way to achieve the American dream. Jobs are scarce for someone who wasn't an "American," and opening a small piece of home provides a means of steady income not only for themselves but also for family members and other immigrants. Plus, if you hire family, overhead costs are reduced. Things were no different in Tucson. As waves of people from Europe and then Asia, the Middle East and Africa arrived, so did the foods of their countries.

Italian

Paesano's

Damiano Ali and his family had been living in Tucson for several years by the time his brother Cosmo moved to town with his small family. Back in Calabria, Italy, their family owned a little store and restaurant, so it was only natural for them to open a restaurant here.

They started with a little spot near the University of Arizona and called it Paesano's Pizzeria. The space had been a diner of sorts, serving American-style breakfast, lunch and dinner. The Alis kept the fare and three-meal-a-day menu for a while, but then they started serving the food they knew best:

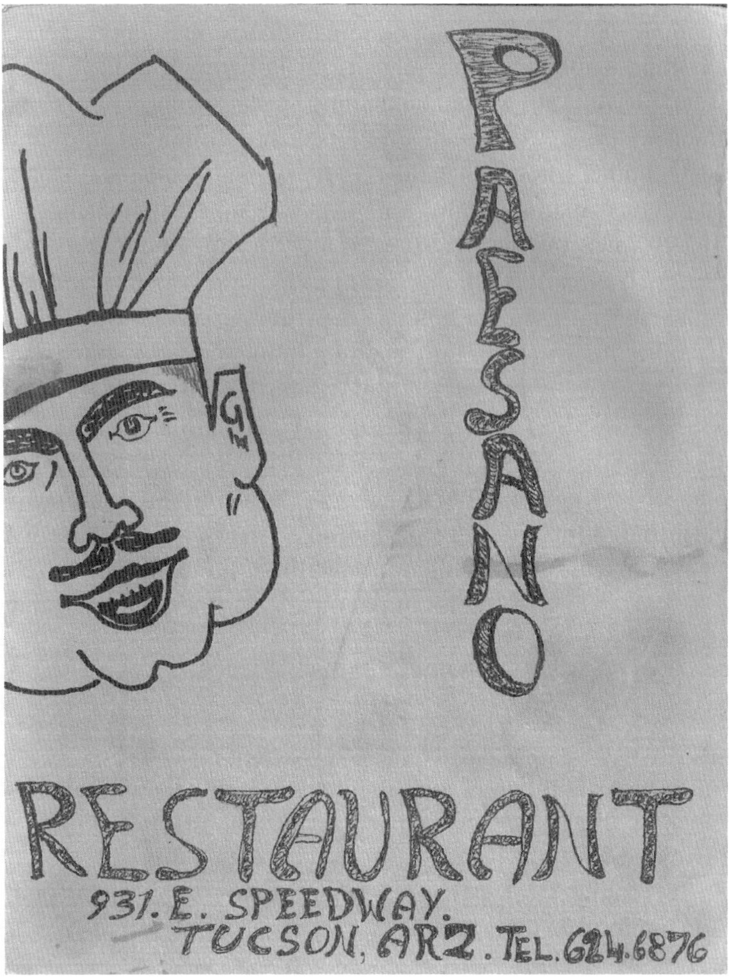

The artwork of Damiano Ali, a hand-drawn menu from Paesano's. *The Ali family.*

pizza with all sorts of toppings, pastas of every kind and, because many customers were college students, submarine sandwiches.[127]

Damiano was an artist, and he designed and drew the menu, with a cheerful chef on the front and artful hand lettering inside. The place was small and dark but welcoming, and the brothers, their wives and young children attracted students and faculty alike. Cosmo's daughter, Pina Colosimo, remembered sitting in the back part of the room and folding pizza boxes with her sister Loretta and her cousins.[128] Former customers,

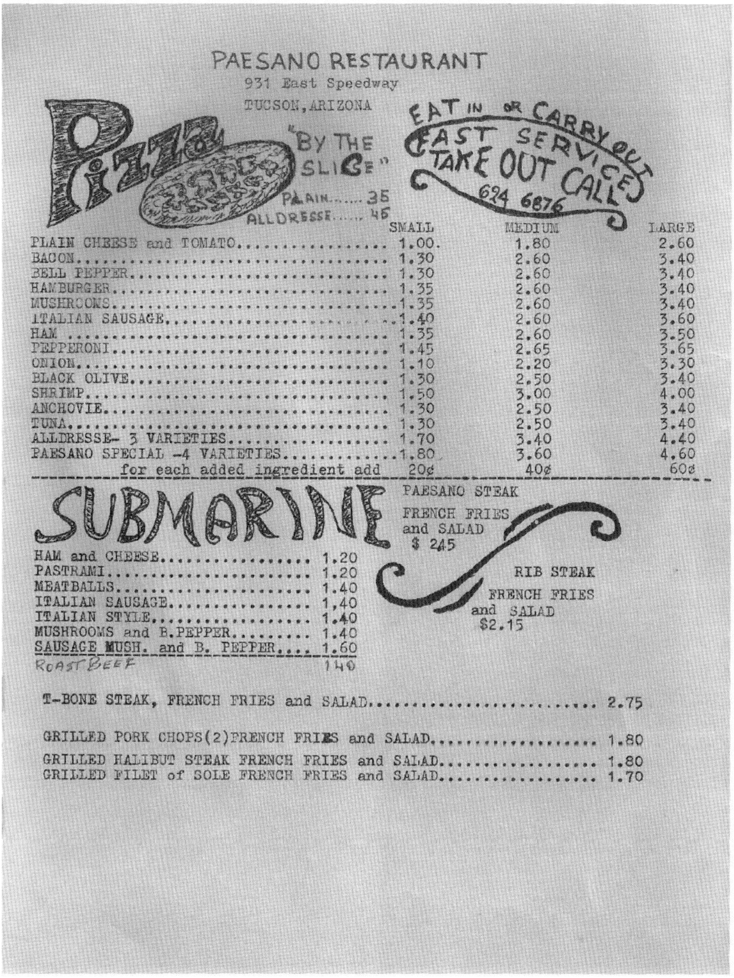

PAESANO RESTAURANT
931 East Speedway
TUCSON, ARIZONA

Pizza "BY THE SLICE" PLAIN...... 35 ALLDRESSE...... 45

EAT IN or CARRY OUT
FAST SERVICE
TAKE OUT CALL
624 6876

	SMALL	MEDIUM	LARGE
PLAIN CHEESE and TOMATO	1.00.	1.80	2.60
BACON	1.30	2.60	3.40
BELL PEPPER	1.30	2.60	3.40
HAMBURGER	1.35	2.60	3.40
MUSHROOMS	1.35	2.60	3.40
ITALIAN SAUSAGE	1.40	2.60	3.60
HAM	1.35	2.60	3.50
PEPPERONI	1.45	2.65	3.65
ONION	1.10	2.20	3.30
BLACK OLIVE	1.30	2.50	3.40
SHRIMP	1.50	3.00	4.00
ANCHOVIE	1.30	2.50	3.40
TUNA	1.30	2.50	3.40
ALLDRESSE- 3 VARIETIES	1.70	3.40	4.40
PAESANO SPECIAL -4 VARIETIES	1.80	3.60	4.60
for each added ingredient add	20¢	40¢	60¢

SUBMARINE

HAM and CHEESE	1.20
PASTRAMI	1.20
MEATBALLS	1.40
ITALIAN SAUSAGE	1,40
ITALIAN STYLE	1.40
MUSHROOMS and B.PEPPER	1.40
SAUSAGE MUSH. and B. PEPPER	1.60
ROAST BEEF	140

PAESANO STEAK
FRENCH FRIES
and SALAD
$ 245

RIB STEAK
FRENCH FRIES
and SALAD
$2.15

T-BONE STEAK, FRENCH FRIES and SALAD	2.75
GRILLED PORK CHOPS(2)FRENCH FRIES and SALAD	1.80
GRILLED HALIBUT STEAK FRENCH FRIES and SALAD	1.80
GRILLED FILET of SOLE FRENCH FRIES and SALAD	1.70

The inside of Paesano's menu. *The Ali family.*

many of them starving students, remembered eating there and having plates refilled in a huge show of generosity and caring.

But then, in 1973, Cosmo and Damiano went their separate ways, each opening his own place. Cosmo opened a tiny spot in midtown and called it DaVinci's. Damiano headed not too far away but in the other direction and called his place, appropriately enough, Damiano's. The parting was amicable, and both restaurants went on to many successful years in the business.

DaVinci's

"It smells like Italy," said a longtime fan who had spent years in Italy while in the air force. He was talking about DaVinci's.[129] Indeed, DaVinci's was a slice of Italy, and for more than twenty-eight years (it opened in 1976), Cosmo and his wife, Anna, welcomed guests with open arms and big plates of pasta, pizza and other Italian specialties. They spoke little English, but that didn't stop them. Both worked day and night, spending most of their time at the restaurant.

They started out with one small room. The chairs were plastic and the décor minimal. But people loved the food, and little by little they added a room here and a room there. They added statuary and murals, plants and columns. Even the chairs were upgraded to red leatherette. In the front waiting area, they built a display case that was filled with Cosmo's handmade desserts. The tiramisu was a specialty. Cosmo had brought the recipe back from Italy. He added a few of his own touches. It became a signature dish.[130]

Everybody worked. Cosmo stayed mostly in the back. Anna cooked and waited tables, and their two daughters were kept busy doing everything from hosting to bussing to folding more of those pizza boxes. "My dad was strict, a perfectionist," Pina said. "My mom was more easygoing. It was a nice balance."

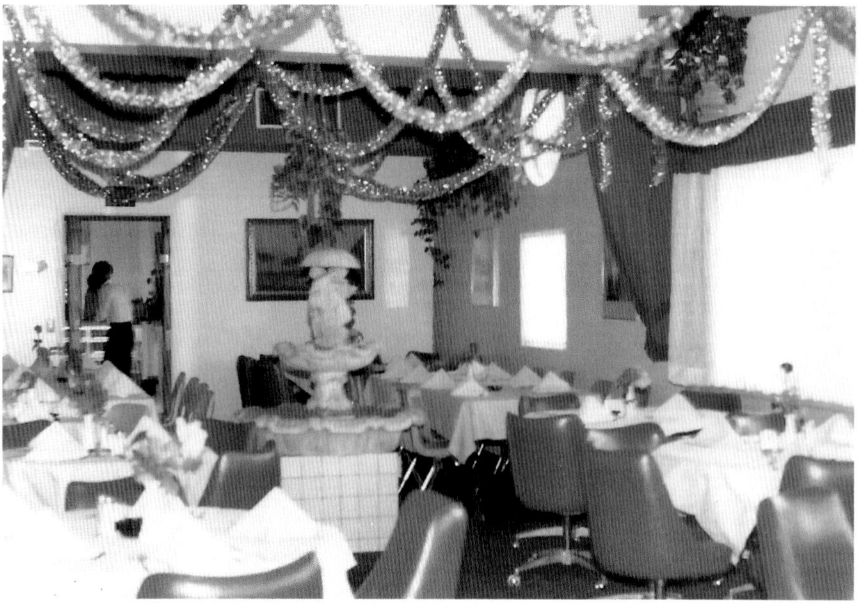

Interior of DaVinci's. *Pina Colosimo.*

On weekend evenings, it wasn't uncommon for customers to wait an hour or more (even in the expanded place), but nobody seemed to mind. They knew that the wait would result in a fabulous meal with leftovers. Cosmo made the gnocchi by hand, and it, along with the pizza, was a popular dish. On Thursday nights, the specialty was the chicken Toscanini, chicken breasts in a white lemon cream sauce with mushrooms and artichoke hearts. As if that wasn't enough to satisfy, it was served with tortellini. Seafood also shone. The seafood risotto was a huge mound of creamy rice with all sorts of seafood. Another seafood treat was the sfoglio, a mix of frutti de mare wrapped and cooked in aluminum foil. And of course, there was that glorious tiramisu. "It was his passion," said Pina.

When Cosmo had a stroke in 2004, it was a sad time for both guests and the family. They sold the place with the name, and then, like so many other former family restaurants, the new owners ran it into the ground. Fortunately for Tucsonans, Pina has her own restaurant called Tratorria Pina. Much like her parents, she works the house with her husband. Cosmo still comes in and makes the gnocchi and that rich, creamy tiramisu.

Damiano's

Damiano and Assunta built a small slump-block building in busy Stone Avenue close enough to the university so their fans could follow them yet far enough away to attract a larger audience. Again Damiano designed the menu, adding pictures of famous Italian sites such as the Leaning Tower of Pisa. He also created signs for each of the daily specials and hung them on the walls.[131]

On Wednesdays, the special was gnocchi with meatballs. On Friday, there were two: either a perch filet served with spaghetti or linguini profumo de bosco e mare. The Saturday night special was an original creation called bucatini dell Lisa ("mushrooms, red or white and a veal cutlet"). Everything came with a choice of soup or salad, a roll and coffee or tea. "Mostly it was him and me. We did everything," said Assunta. Their sons each started working at the restaurant as soon as they were old enough.

Soon they added other rooms to the long, narrow space, eventually adding a separate room for the bar. There were tables and booths with red-checked tablecloths. There was a stone wall waterfall and a beautiful stone fountain. At lunch, lawyers, police officers, business people and government officials would make the short drive from

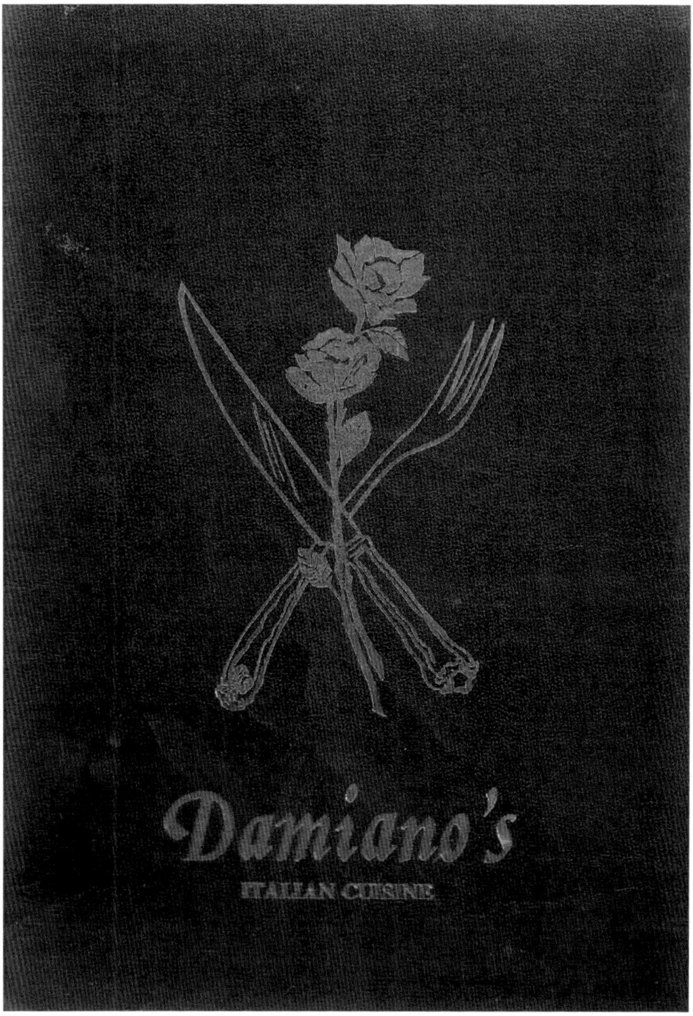

Damiano's goes uptown with this elite menu, but the artwork is still by Damiano Ali. *The Ali family.*

downtown to enjoy an authentic Italian meal. At dinner, families would come. The prices were so reasonable and the portions so big that a family could eat well and bring home leftovers.

Regulars included Michael Landon when he was in town filming *Little House on the Prairie* or for his annual tennis tournament. Son Vince remembered Lee Marvin driving up in a "raggedy old truck. He kept to himself." The singer Mark Lindsay and actor Slim Pickens were also regulars.[132]

Like his brother, Damiano was stern and a perfectionist. But the family has many photos of him enjoying good times with family and guests. Sundays were family times. Everyone got together to cook, eat and relax.

As the business expanded, so did the menu. Several steaks were added; veal choices included the usual items and house creations "alla Damiano." Another house specialty was the Italian Combination alla Assunta, which included lasagna, cannelloni and manicotti topped with sauce and mozzarella cheese. No one ever walked away from the table hungry.

They sold the business lock, stock and barrel in 1985 to two men from India and moved to the then relatively quiet northwest side, opening Michelangelo's. "My dad took chances," said Vince. "I think that's one reason why we are still here."[133] The family still gets together on Sundays. It is a little larger, but other than that, not much has changed.

Fiorito's

Fiorito's was the very definition of a nice little neighborhood place. Located in midtown on busy Grant Road, Fiorito's was first owned by Vern and Mary Lou Lowe. The Lowes brought family recipes from Chicago around 1988. Not much is known about the Lowes, but they sold the place to Tess O'Shea and her husband, John Burke, in 1999. Both O'Shea and Burke had been involved in the restaurant scene in Tucson for many years, and they were looking for a place just like Fiorito's.[134]

They spiffed up the dining room and kitchen a little bit and added some fancier items to the menu, but basically they kept many of the Lowes' recipes, in particular the pizza. Pizza was at the very core of the food at Fiorito's. Both traditional and deep dish were served, and the toppings ranged from the usual, like sausage and pepperoni, to a little more creative items, such as bay shrimp and artichokes.[135]

Fiorito's was the first place in town to serve white pizza. It was topped with mozzarella, Romano, ricotta and provolone cheeses; a dash of fresh tomato; scallions; olive oil; and garlic. The aroma was heavenly. The flavors were unlike anything else found in Tucson.

O'Shea and Burke used Mary Lou's recipes for meatballs, Italian beef sandwiches, cheesecake and more, but fennel braised lamb shanks in red wine also played a starring role. The veal piccata rivaled any found at the more upscale, expensive places in town. The wine list was small but smart.

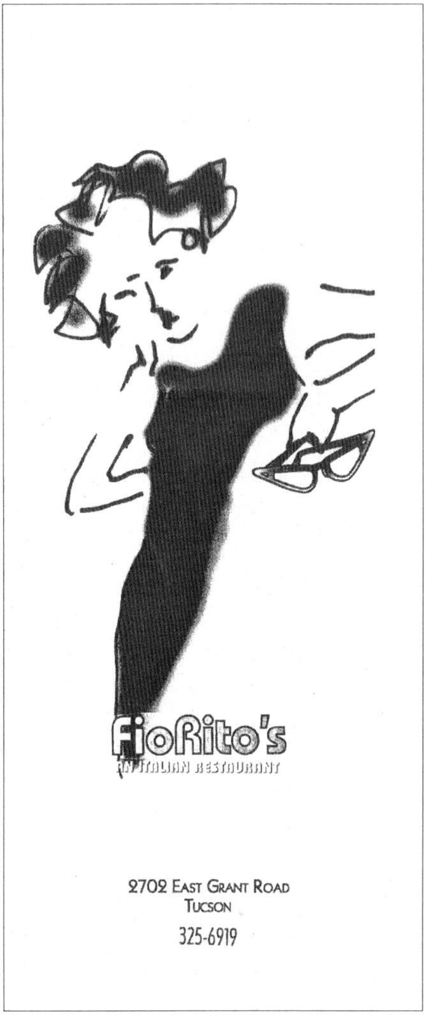

Fiorito's, your friendly little neighborhood Italian joint. *Author's collection.*

People remember the food there, but what seems to stick in most people's memories is the warm, cozy atmosphere. Families could feel welcome there, but Fiorito's was also very romantic. Regulars, and there were many of them, knew to get to Fiorito's early to avoid having to wait for a table.

There was a bar, which was used mostly by people waiting for a pizza to go (there also was a drive-through window). The tables were situated close together and covered in white tablecloths. Candles and a small bouquet of fresh flowers sat on every table, along with bottles of olive oil and balsamic vinegar for dipping bread. But the prime seats were the booths, especially those along the outside wall. Curtains hung in the windows, shielding diners from all the traffic that was whizzing by on Grant Road just a few feet away. But the atmosphere was so intimate that you would never really know the outside world existed.

O'Shea and Burke sold Fiorito's in 2004. But when the city announced that Grant Road would be widened, the new owner opted out and closed the place without notice in 2010.[136]

Chinese

Tucson had its fair share of Chinese restaurants. They were neighborhood places, most of which have faded into obscurity. Others remain stubbornly open, which is a good thing.

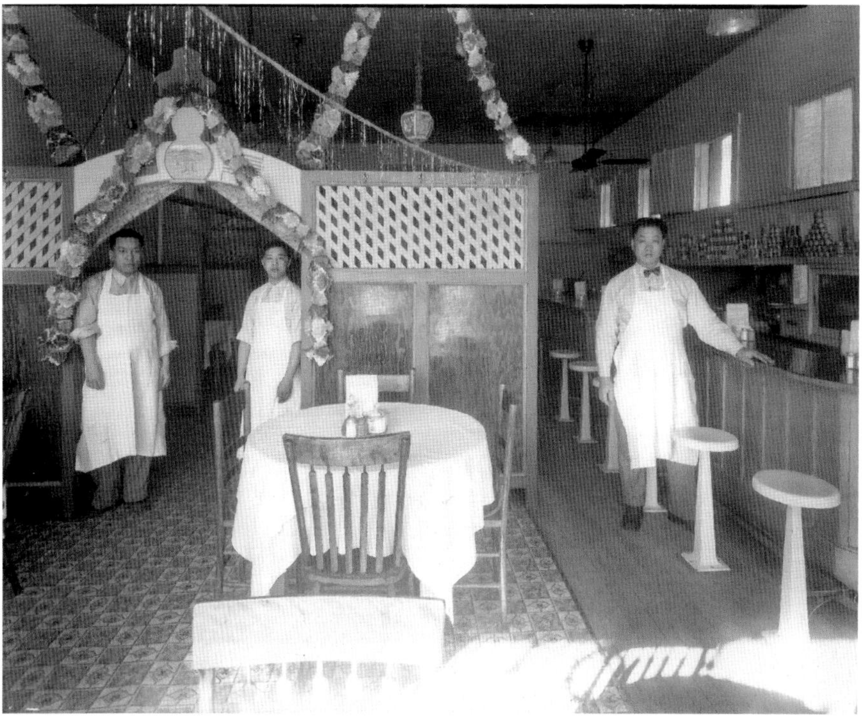

The Richilieu was run by a Chinese family and was considered to be quite refined. *Arizona Historical Society*.

Jerry's Ming House

In spite of the fact that everyone we spoke to remembers Jerry's Ming House, there isn't much information to be found on the popular restaurant. People have vague but very personal memories of the place. One gentleman remembered the really inexpensive egg rolls (which made this place very popular with him and his friends, who were students at the nearby University of Arizona). Another contact remembered going there with her parents; because she didn't like Chinese food, she always had a grilled cheese sandwich.

A postcard shows booths and white tablecloths, as well as big Chinese lanterns hanging from the ceiling. Shades of red and black dominate. Lee's nephew, Danny Lee, said that the card is very representative of how the dining room looked. But his memories are as hazy as the others. He knows that his uncle owned Jerry Lee Ho Market in Barrio Viejo prior to opening the restaurant, but he doesn't know when he closed the market and

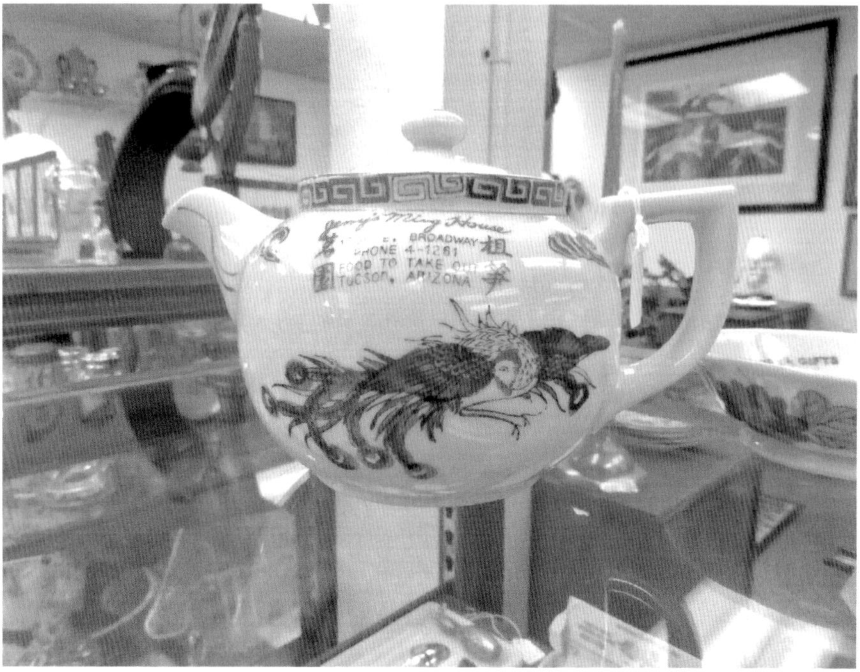

A teapot from Jerry Ming's House. American Antique Mall. *Author's collection.*

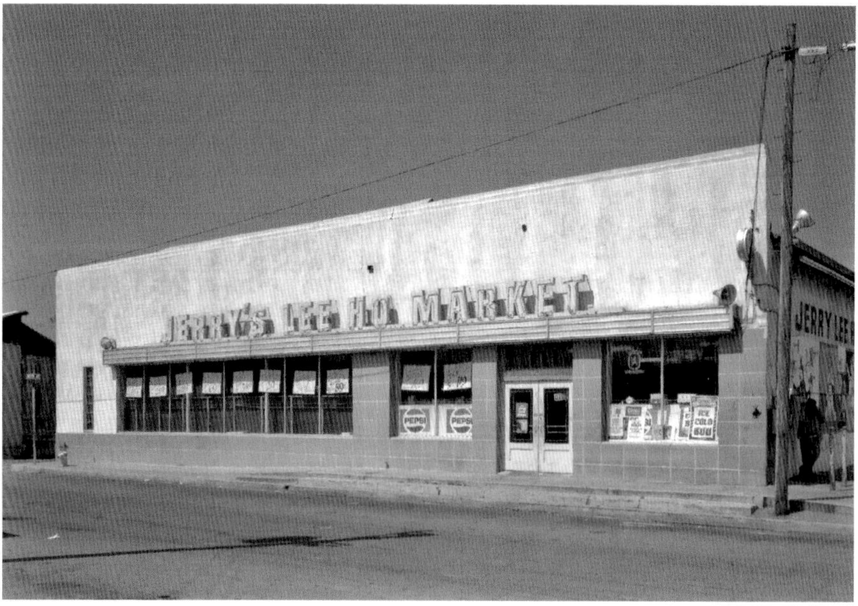

Jerry's Lee Ho Market. Jerry Lee purchased the business prior to owning his popular restaurant. *Library of Congress.*

opened the restaurant. He remembered reading about his uncle being in a devastating car accident in 1953.[137]

He said the restaurant was a center for the Chinese community; it was the site of the Lee Family Association dinners, where all the families named Lee would meet regularly. On the Fourth of July, Jerry Lee and another restaurant owner, also named Lee, would cook mountains of fried chicken for the entire Chinese community.[138]

Yet the dining room was always busy with non-Asians. Dr. "Big Jim" Griffith said that he doesn't ever remember eating at any other Chinese restaurant in Tucson. The menu was "tamed down" for the Caucasian palate. Danny Lee's favorite dish? The Chinese barbecue ribs, which were bright red in color. Jerry Lee taught Chinese cooking classes at Pima Community College in 1972. Danny Lee estimated that Jerry's Ming House probably closed in the late 1970s.

Golden Pagoda

While Jerry Ming's House was elegant and roomy, the Golden Pagoda on Grant Road was completely the opposite. The room held about ten unadorned tables, and the kitchen was open and noisy. It was the very essence of a mom and pop restaurant. It was run by David So for thirty years. So sold it to another family (name unknown), who ran it from 1982 to 1987—"the whole family was there to help."[139]

VIETNAMESE

Three Sisters

In the early '80s, Chinese food was the only Asian food found in Tucson. Be Scott, Le Tran and Mai Tran were three sisters from Vietnam and wanted to bring the flavors of their homeland to Tucson. Starting with a food truck, which they parked in an industrial section of the west side, the sisters started dishing out plate after plate of traditional Vietnamese fare. Be's daughter, Kim Moran, remembered sleeping in the truck while the sisters cooked.[140]

Soon they had enough money to open a freestanding restaurant. Located not far from the original site of the truck, the Three Sisters opened in 1984. The neighborhood was a mix of motorcycle shops, roofing companies and garages. There was a small parking lot in front. They served both Chinese and Vietnamese food to attract customers, but once people tried the Vietnamese dishes, they were hooked. The multi-leveled room was lined in bamboo, with palm trees and big mahogany bar that served "Polynesian"-style drinks.

Many of the dishes were original recipes straight out of the women's mother's kitchen in Vietnam. She also had lush greenhouse where, among other things, she grew mint, traditional squashes, lemongrass, limes and the fire-hot Thai chiles used in making nuoc cham, Vietnamese garlic chile sauce.

One of her creations came from having friends in Vietnam who were Buddhist monks and vegetarians. It was called Cauliflower Delight. The sisters mixed thinly sliced cauliflower with sliced almonds and coconut and then pan-fried them like little pancakes. It was served with the nuoc cham. They were heavenly and could turn anyone into a cauliflower lover.[141]

Another popular dish was called Imperial Beef (or Chicken). Grape leaves were stuffed with minced meat seasoned with lemongrass and garlic and then rolled. It was served with an assortment of cilantro, carrots, rice noodles and other goodies. You would then roll the items in rice paper. The fish soup was also a big hit.

The family also operated Asian Art and Food, a specialty store on Speedway. When the new owners of the motorcycle shop next door caused issues with parking and noise, the three sisters closed Three Sisters. Mai had married and wanted to start a family, so Be and Le moved north and opened Mekong restaurant.[142] Mekong was popular but eventually closed, due in part, Moran believes, to the influx of chains that dumbed down the palates of the customers.

French

French restaurants are few and far between in Tucson's culinary history. Those that did open seemed to close quickly, but two, Penelope's and Le Bistro, made their marks.

Penelope's

In its twenty years of operation, under three ownerships, Penelope's gave Tucsonans a taste of France and, to be honest, taught Tucsonans the finer points of cuisine François. It was originally located in an old house on Speedway Boulevard near Alvernon Road, close enough to both the university and midtown middle-class neighborhoods to attract a nice crowd.

Penelope's first owner was Penelope Miedaner. Her approach was country French. Her menu was small, as was her kitchen, but she grew the business and developed a loyal group of customers.[113] Miedaner ran the place for about six years and then sold it to a couple who, after about a year, sold it to Dr. Patricia Sparks. And it was under Sparks that Penelope's became a go-to place to dine.

Sparks was originally from Maryland and lived in Chicago before moving to Tucson to run Penelope's. While working the restaurant, she finished her studies at the University of Arizona, earning a PhD in nutritional science.[114] At the time she took over reins, the kitchen at Penelope's was pretty much the kitchen that had been in the original house. She had a four-burner residential stove and used a toaster oven to cook such dishes as her famous French onion soup and escargot. Little by little, she converted the space into a more workable area.

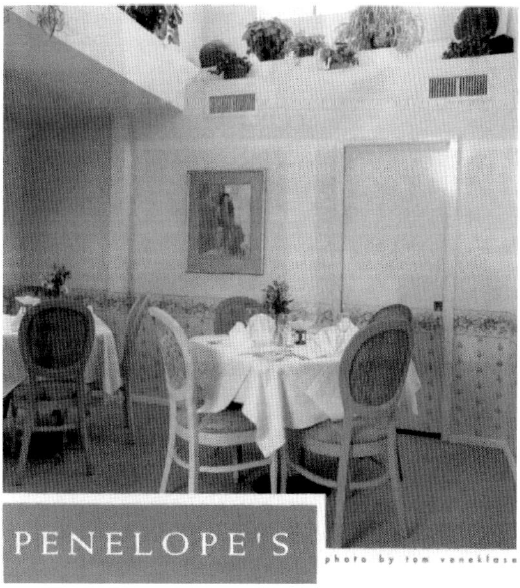

The interior of Penelope's. Photo by Tim Veneklasen. *Dr. Patricia Spark.*

Under Sparks's fine hand, dinner was a *prix fixe* menu, something almost unheard of in Tucson. The menu changed every two weeks. There were six courses; wine was extra. She also hosted weekly wine dinners in the fall that highlighted various regions of France. Appetizers could be a pâté or a salmon mousse. This was followed by potage (soup), which was either the French onion (one of the few items that was always on the menu) or some other soup. Vichyssoise was the perfect foil to the summer heat of Tucson. This was followed by the choice of one of four entrées (with filet mignon also being a permanent item). Then, in the French fashion, salad followed. Dessert was next; if diners were lucky, Sparks would be serving her signature black-and-white chocolate mousse torte. Finally, cheese would be served.[145]

In 1992, the city widened Speedway, and Penelope's was shuttered. Within a year, it reopened on Swan Road. It took considerable work to clean up the grounds, but Sparks and her crew turned the area into a lovely garden setting where many weddings and other special occasions were held.[146]

Both locals and visitors became regulars at Penelope's. They loved the pure French flavors and Sparks's warm hospitality. Sparks closed the restaurant in 1998. These days, she teaches food sciences at the university and runs a midtown bed-and-breakfast called Mon Ami. There guests can still enjoy many of the dishes that made Penelope's so popular for all those twenty years.

Greek and Mediterranean

Le Mediterranean

Most family restaurants get their recipes from mothers and grandmothers and even some times grandfathers, but the recipes found at Le Mediterranean date back some eight hundred years. Joe Abi-Ad was born in Lebanon, and when he came to Tucson in 1976, he brought with him century-old recipes. He said that his family had been in the food business for centuries, and he used these recipes at his first restaurant, the Rubiyat.[147] When he and his wife, Jacqueline, opened Le Mediterranean in 1993, he continued to use these same recipes, much to the delight of Tucson diners, although few probably knew their ancient roots.

Lamb was central to the menu at Le Mediterranean, which was located on Sabino Canyon and Snyder Roads. Lamb shank, leg of lamb and lamb chops were offered every night. The lamb shank, one of the best items on the menu, was marinated and then slow-cooked for hours. Abi-Ad said that it was so tender you didn't even need a knife.[148]

The chicken shawarma was also popular, and as fitting at any true Mediterranean restaurant, there were many vegetarian items available as well. Sides included basmati rice and couscous. Desserts included interesting takes on baklava, such as using pine nuts instead of pistachios. The wines were from Lebanon. Beer was also available. On Friday and Saturday nights, there were belly dancers.

When George Clooney came to the area to film *Three Kings*, Joe and Jacqueline got speaking parts. Pictures of their touch with Hollywood can be found on the walls of Joe's Pancake House, the restaurant that Abi-Ad has run for thirty years. Le Mediterranean was extremely popular, but a new landlord forced Joe out in 2002. Joe opened a fast-casual restaurant for several years, but these days, he can always be found at the Pancake House.

El Greco/El Greco Grecian Gardens

Many people remember El Greco as a hole-in-the-wall university-area spot where you could get a bowl of avgolemono soup or a souvlaki plate for a couple of dollars. Others remember a more elegant dining space on Fort Lowell Road where there was quiet table service and wine. Either way, the food was great.

Ptolemeos Kotzambsis, whom everyone called Pete, and his wife, Lois, ran the university El Greco for twenty years. The room was small and lined with wooden benches. Rustic, yes, but it allowed diners to watch the cooks slice strips of gyro meat for sandwiches and see the flames that charred the souvlaki. If you were feeling flush, you could order a slice of baklava to round out your meal. El Greco was one of the places that the university commandeered in the name of expansion, so the Kotzambsises moved north to a quiet building on Fort Lowell Road.[149]

Arches and murals of Greece and white tablecloths almost required a fancier name, and so El Greco became El Greco Grecian Gardens. The menu was expanded to include squid, lamb, flaming cheese and more sweet Greek desserts. The name was different, the décor was certainly different (there was even a fountain!) and the clientele had a little more money, but El Greco was essentially the same. Pete and Lois closed El Greco Grecian Gardens in 2005.

The Olive Tree

From an interview with Michael "Benny" Benedetto, July 2015.

The Olive Tree could easily find a place in other sections of this book, but because it served the epitome of Greek food in Tucson, it's tucked into this chapter. The Olive Tree's roots began at another popular Greek restaurant, Gyro Taverna, which was located in La Placita Plaza downtown. Gyro Taverna was immensely popular, but then owner/manager John Condiss decided to open a larger place that offered a more upscale feel.

Condiss was a Greek American who came from Chicago. He worked on the City of Tucson Police Department and was a member of Tucson's original SWAT team. Running a restaurant might have seemed easy after that. So, in 1978, he and wife Leslie headed east and opened the Olive Tree on Tanque Verde Road. It immediately became one of the most popular restaurants on Restaurant Row; in fact, the Olive Tree became one of the most popular restaurants in the city. Their dream was to create excellent Greek food, and they did so for thirty years.

"We were extremely busy right off the bat," said Michael "Benny" Benedetto, who had worked with Condiss at Gyro Taverna. He and a handful of the Taverna staff followed Condiss to the bigger digs. It speaks volumes that most stayed with them for the majority of the time the restaurant was open.[150]

A regular crowd stayed with them as well, said Benedetto, who worked his way up from young waiter to manager. He recalled people coming in from big cities—New York, Chicago, Los Angeles and beyond—and telling him that the Olive Tree was the best Greek restaurant in the country. The national press agreed. In 1991, *Fortune* magazine called the Olive Tree the "Best Greek Restaurant in the West," and the *New York Times* proclaimed it to be "A must restaurant to visit in Tucson." It was featured in *Bon Appétit* magazine, as well.

While the food won kudos, Benedetto credited the Condisses' management style for much of the success. "They demanded without demanding. They took care of the staff, which is why the staff worked hard for them," he said. That care was demonstrated when a fire closed the restaurant for a month in 1991. Condiss continued to pay the staff their wages, including tips, through the month that it took to repair the damage.[151]

The staff wore white shirts, black pants, black shoes, a cummerbund and a tie. They were elegant, attentive and well loved by the customers. They were a tight group, which, Benedetto said, made working and dining at the Olive Tree extra special.

The menu had all the traditional Greek dishes: flaming saganaki, moussaka, spanakopita and dolmathas. And there were the house specialties, like the Spartan salad, which combined greens, avocado, green peppers, tomatoes and onions tossed in a feta dressing and topped with grilled shrimp.[152] Lamb dishes shone. The Lamb Bandit came from a story that Condiss read about bandits who lived in the hills of old Greece. They would steal a lamb from nearby farmers, slaughter it, mix the meat with whatever vegetables they had on hand and then wrap it all in the stomach of the lamb. It was then cooked on coals rather than a big fire that might attract the law. Condiss used aluminum foil and cooked the dish for three or four hours in the oven. The Lamb Bandit was one of the most requested dishes on the menu. Chef Cliff Ball, who worked with Condiss in the kitchen for twenty-two years, also made fantastic fish dishes, steaks and other American plates.[153]

Regular customers sometimes ate there two or three times a week, Benedetto recalled. Some didn't even need a menu. The staff knew what they wanted, and the kitchen produced it. Regulars included state Supreme Court judges, University of Arizona basketball coach Lute Olsen and a woman who drove down from Scottsdale every Wednesday for lunch. Staff members from other restaurants ate there on a regular basis as well, which in the restaurant business is a huge compliment. When The Tack Room won many of its yearly awards, staff would go to the Olive Tree to celebrate.

John and Leslie divorced but remained business partners and good friends, and the restaurant continued to be the place to go to for Greek food and a relaxed evening. Then, in 2008, the Tucson economy hit a snag. The state also enacted a smoking ban, which hit the Olive Tree hard. Condiss estimated that he was losing $15,000 a month on liquor sales alone due to the ban. Gas prices were high, and the minimum wage was raised. Things were stacking up against Condiss and other restaurant owners. In 2008, the *Tucson Citizen* listed forty-two restaurant closures, which included everything from upscale restaurants to down-home barbecue joints and drive-ins. No one ever openly said that this unusually high number of closures was due to the ban, but certainly the Olive Tree was not the only restaurant that suffered from the law.[154]

The decision to close was not an easy one. After all, thirty years is a long run with such a successful restaurant like the Olive Tree.

Soul Food Supreme

Art's BBQ & Velda's Catering

Art and Velda Fluellen moved to Tucson from North Carolina without any real experience in running a restaurant, but the little hole-in-the-wall

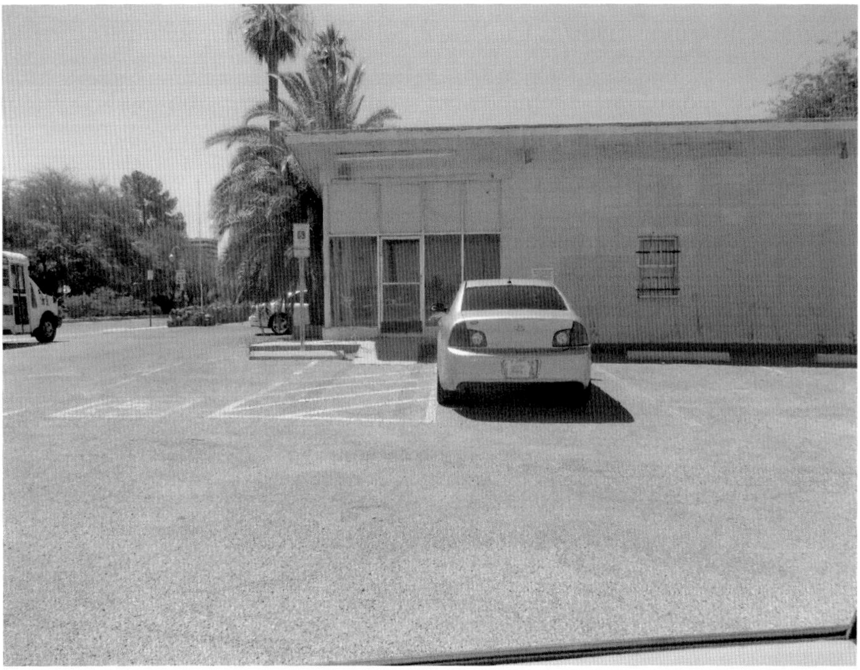

The site of Art's BBQ. The building has sat empty since it closed in 2008. *Author's collection.*

barbecue restaurant that they in opened in 1995 was extremely popular for fourteen years. Art had worked for IBM, and Velda had taught biochemistry, but when friends encouraged them to share Velda's cooking with others, they decided to go for it. They started with a catering company.

Located halfway between downtown and the west side, Art's BBQ attracted a mixed but steady crowd of customers. Art did all the smoking (twelve hours or more), and on most days, he could be found in the cozy dining room keeping an eye on things. There were small notices about Vietnam vets quietly displayed in the place; if Art was a vet himself, diners never knew.[155]

Art was the meat man, but it was Velda who spooned out helpings of savory meats, homemade sides and memorable desserts, all with a side of "honey" and "dear." The meats were dark and lush, and their smoky aroma followed you out the door. Sides were made with recipes from Velda's mother's kitchen. Cooking was done the only way she knew how, with love and passion. Healthy eating was also essential, Velda noted in an interview in 2008, so she fried food in canola oil, even the hush puppies. Her hush puppies were to die for; sometimes she would come out of the kitchen and give customers several samples of the tasty treats "just because."

It was almost impossible to not have dessert at Art's because you ordered at the counter, where Velda displayed all her homemade items. Then, as you made your way through the ribs or chicken or pulled pork sandwich, they seemed to call to you. Like everything else at Art's, the desserts were homemade by Velda.

Like with many other restaurants, progress got in the way of Art's. The land was owned by the State of Arizona Department of Transportation, and in 2008, the state put it up for sale. A plan to build a parkway had changed, and the state no longer needed the lot. As of today, the lot and building are bare. The Fluellens opted out of buying the site and closed Art's later that year, although the catering business continued for a while[156]

Jack's Original BBQ

Jack's was the go-to place for barbecue for many years. What began as a little joint on Grant Road grew to be a little joint on Twenty-second Street. In its time, Jack's closed and opened and then closed and opened, finally closing the doors in 2014.

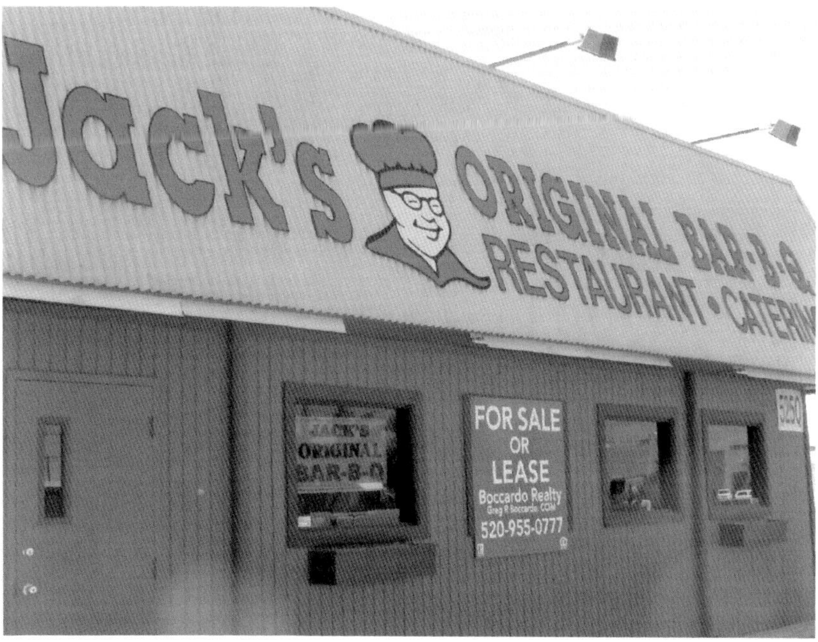

Jack's was the "ORIGINAL" barbecue. *Author's collection.*

The "original" Jack was Jack Banks, who opened the business in 1950 and ran it until 1988. His wife, Laura, was a big part of the business. It was the longest-run African American business in Tucson.[157] People said it was the sauce that made Jack's so unique. Most of the business was takeout, but Jack's was always busy.

Due to ill health, Banks sold his business—with the name intact—to Hortense Hayes. Hortense was a lawyer from Chicago who had eaten at Jack's and had loved it and even thought about buying it. On another visit, she ran into Laura. Laura mentioned that they were selling the business, and Hayes decided to go for it. She took over in 1986.[158] She kept many of the same recipes, but in 1988, she lost the restaurant to bankruptcy. It was then that the Bankses stepped in and "reopened" their own restaurant, only to sell it to the Boccardo family, who ran it for fifteen years. The economy hit the Boccardos hard, and they closed Jack's in 2012.[159] Then James and Sylvia Williams opened Jack's, but their ownership lasted only a few years.

These days, the building sits empty, waiting for someone else to fire up the barbecue. Odds are slim that that will ever happen.

Big Al's BBQ

Big Al's claim to fame, aside from the ribs and chicken and peach cobbler, came in 1974, when a young director by the name of Martin Scorsese filmed the "little" movie *Alice Doesn't Live Here Anymore* at Big Al's. In the movie, Big Al's became Mel's, and the barbecue menu was shelved. But Big Al's will forever be remembered as "that restaurant in Tucson where Martin Scorsese made a movie." The restaurant plays a central role in the movie, as that's where Alice stops to make some money on her way to Sacramento and her lifelong dream of a singing career. She meets her true love (played by Kris Kristofferson) there and raises her son, Tommy, at the attached motel. Ellen Burstyn won an Academy Award for Best Actress, and Jodie Foster had a small role.

But the food here shone as bright as any Hollywood star. The building was circular, with big windows wrapping around all but the back wall. Not that there was much to see, as the neighborhood was mostly small industry sites. Big Al Fowler worked the pass, dishing up fall-apart ribs with his homemade sauce. There was a fish fry on Fridays that had people waiting in line for a table. You had to get there early if you wanted a piece of cobbler.

At one time, the building was the site of Duke's Drive-in. Sometime in the 1960s, Duke leased the place to Fowler, who changed the name and got rid of the drive-in part. Fowler was the first African American in Tucson to obtain a federal small business loan.[160]

Big Al's closed sometime in the 1980s. The building stands today and is a bar and nightclub, appropriately called the Beau Brummel Club.

Feig's Kosher deli was Tucson's only 100 percent kosher deli for sixty-five years until it closed in 2008.

Chapter 6

Cafés, Drive-ins and Everything in Between

The sad part about shuttered cafeterias, cafés, ice cream parlors and drive-ins is that many of them, no matter how popular they were, have simply disappeared. Trying to find information about them is almost impossible. The only things left are a couple memories here and there, but nothing specific about the owners, the food or the history.

Kippy's Burgers is a prime example. People talk about the takeout bags of burgers that were soaked with a greasy goodness by time they got home, but that's about all the information found. The Central Dryve-in, which was located on Speedway and Stone, was torn down to make way for a burger chain, which is itself long gone. Several people mentioned the Central, but any paperwork or photos are nonexistent. When the city enacted a smoking ban in 1999, Molly G's Diner found a way to get around it by becoming a "Private Dining Club." It charged one dollar to join, and then you could smoke inside.[161] But again, in spite of this small historic note, little is known about Molly G's. The only thing people remember about Pinkie's Drive-in is the special of ten tacos for one dollar.

Yet all these places were part of Tucson's dining history. Too bad. Memories, faded as they are, are all that's left.

Hamburgers, Hot Rods and Rock-and-Roll

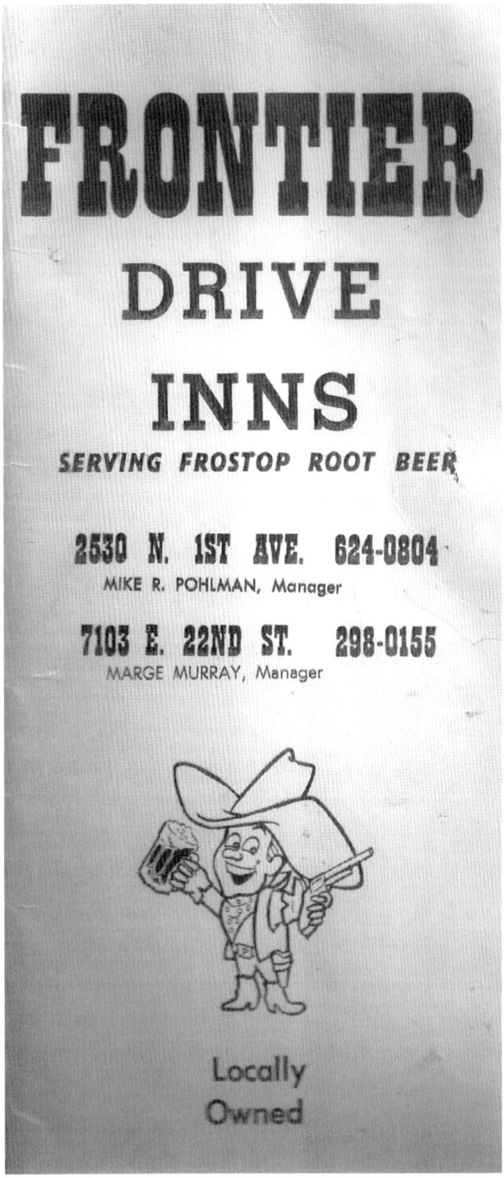

The Frontier Drive-in served ice-cold root beer. *Susan Frank.*

Like any good American city in in mid-twentieth century, Tucson had its fair share of drive-ins. Teens had cars, and cars meant freedom. Freedom to be out on a Friday or Saturday night on your own, without your parents, with your best friends. If you didn't have a car, you knew someone who did.

And everybody needed someplace to go after the football game or the dance in your high school gym. What better place than a drive-in? The food was cheap and greasy good, and the music included the latest hits—maybe you'd also run into that cute guy you saw cruising Speedway.

The rivalries were intense among the high schools in town both on and off the field and were often played out at the drive-in. There were fights and drag races—the Frontier Drive-in had a strict set of rules that included no squealing of tires or horn blowing,[162] but generally a night at your favorite drive-in was a safe time.

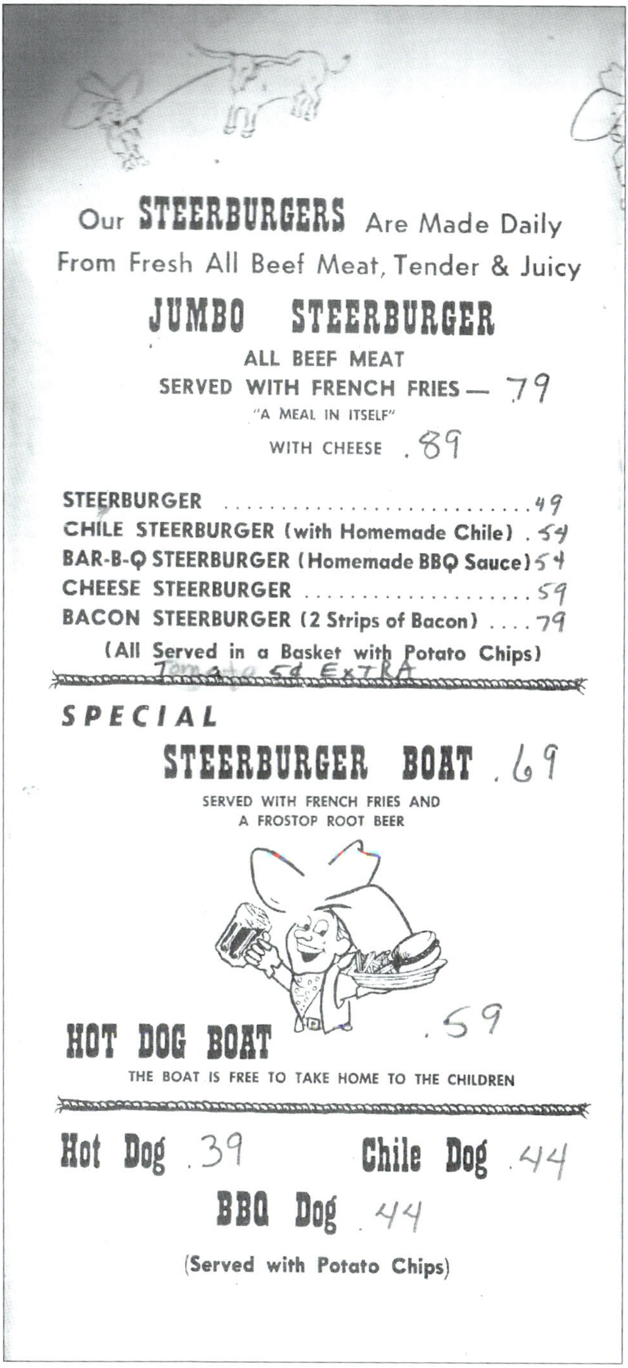

Our STEERBURGERS Are Made Daily
From Fresh All Beef Meat, Tender & Juicy

JUMBO STEERBURGER

ALL BEEF MEAT
SERVED WITH FRENCH FRIES — .79
"A MEAL IN ITSELF"
WITH CHEESE .89

STEERBURGER .... .49
CHILE STEERBURGER (with Homemade Chile) . .54
BAR-B-Q STEERBURGER (Homemade BBQ Sauce) .54
CHEESE STEERBURGER .... .59
BACON STEERBURGER (2 Strips of Bacon) .... .79
(All Served in a Basket with Potato Chips)
Tomato 5¢ EXTRA

SPECIAL

STEERBURGER BOAT .69

SERVED WITH FRENCH FRIES AND
A FROSTOP ROOT BEER

HOT DOG BOAT .59

THE BOAT IS FREE TO TAKE HOME TO THE CHILDREN

Hot Dog .39 Chile Dog .44

BBQ Dog .44

(Served with Potato Chips)

The interior of the Frontier Drive-in menu. *Susan Frank.*

Duke's Drive-in

Duke Shaw ran the only African American restaurant in Tucson in the 1940s and 1950s. You could eat inside or outside. African American professional baseball players would hang out there because the Pioneer Hotel, where the teams stayed, was "white only." They stayed at the attached motel.[163] In 1953, it became the home of the Beau Brummel Club, an exclusive gentlemen's club for young black men. Duke leased the place to Al Fowler, who got the first small business loan from the federal government and opened Big Al's BBQ.[164]

Dixie Drive-in

The Dixie Drive-in was a precursor to many that followed. It was located on Stone Avenue, Tucson's north–south main drag at the time. The Densford family opened the Dixie in the late 1930s. It was open twenty-four hours a day and served a complete three-meal-per-day menu. But the specialty was fried shrimp.[165] Carhops waited on cars outside, but if you wanted a little more refined dining, there was an indoor dining room as well. The Dixie Drive-in closed in the mid-1950s.

The Polar Bar

When Derald Fulton and Paul Shaar opened the Polar Bar on Speedway Boulevard and Country Club Roads, people doubted that they'd make any money way out that way. It was July 2, 1948, and that corner was considered the end of town.[166] But Fulton knew what he was doing; he'd met with great success at a Polar Bar in Phoenix. He hired a few carhops, and within no time at all the lines were out the door (or at least the parking lot was full every night). Fulton and Shaar were making food and money faster than even they could've imagined.

The signature dish was called the Zombie, nearly a quart of ice cream topped with everything but the kitchen sink. People had to pony up one thin dollar for the monstrosity, but no one seemed to mind. For those with a weaker constitution, the menu offered the Sissy Zombie, "twice as little for half as much."[167] Another popular ice cream treat was the Toe Tickler, the Polar Bar's take on a hot fudge sundae.

From the savory side of the menu, people could order the Bellyache, labeled "The World's Largest Sandwich." The only ingredients listed were "old fry cooks and other delicacies." There were burgers, of course, and fried shrimp baskets. But it was the fried chicken that made the Polar Bar famous. It came in three sizes: Jr., Mom and Pop. These days, that same chicken can be found at the Lucky Wishbone restaurants that are located all over Tucson.

Lucky Wishbone was Fulton's next endeavor. The Polar Bar was getting to be more work than it was worth due to teenage fights, rowdy customers and the like. Fulton and his other partners (not Shaar) opened the first Lucky Wishbone on South Sixth Avenue, and the Polar Bar faded into foodie heaven.[168]

Johnie's

Johnie's is one restaurant that came up again and again when I started asking people which restaurants I should include in this book. And it's easy to see why.[169] First of all, there were four Johnie's conveniently located around town. In 1957, there was one on Stone Avenue, which was basically the north side, and another one on Speedway Boulevard, which was home away from home to midtown teens. Then a third Johnie's was built at Twenty-second Street and Alvernon Road, also midtown but a little farther south. And finally, there was a fourth Johnie's on Craycroft Road and Speedway Boulevard, which in 1962 was considered the far east side. This meant that no matter which high school you went to, there was a Johnie's nearby.

Carl Wright purchased the original two Johnie's from Frank Johnson in 1957.[170] The burger here was called the Fat Boy. Favorite drinks were cherry 7 Ups and chocolate Cokes. Other sandwiches included steak sandwiches and shrimp sandwiches. And of course, there were the fries—always the fries. Curb service was the way to go for teenagers, but there was also an indoor dining room. Although Johnie's was open twenty-four hours a day, curb service by law ended around 2:00 a.m. Many a romance started at Johnie's, some of which ended in marriages. These couples later brought their kids to Johnie's, and the legend continued.

Times were hard on the Johnie's restaurants, and slowly, one by one, they closed down.

Shari's

Shari's may not have drawn the crowds that other drive-ins did, but that didn't mean this small spot on First Avenue wasn't popular. And while it began around the same time as all those others (it opened in 1955), Shari's outlasted the best of them, closing in mid-2008.

At first, the only thing that Shari's—then called June's Dairy Delight—served was ice cream, which may account for why the building was built so small. But then, in 1957, burgers were put on the menu, and they remained the mainstay until Shari's final days. The name was officially changed to Shari's in 1979 after Shari Bartol, one of several people who owned the place.[171]

Those burgers were made from fresh ground beef, and in spite of being always served well-done, they were juicy and full of beefy flavor. They came as singles, doubles and even triples, but a double cheeseburger with a side of fries was more than enough to satisfy any hunger. Maybe because of its ice cream parlor roots, milkshakes were also famous here. These shakes were how shakes should be. Like the burgers, they were freshly made. Real ice

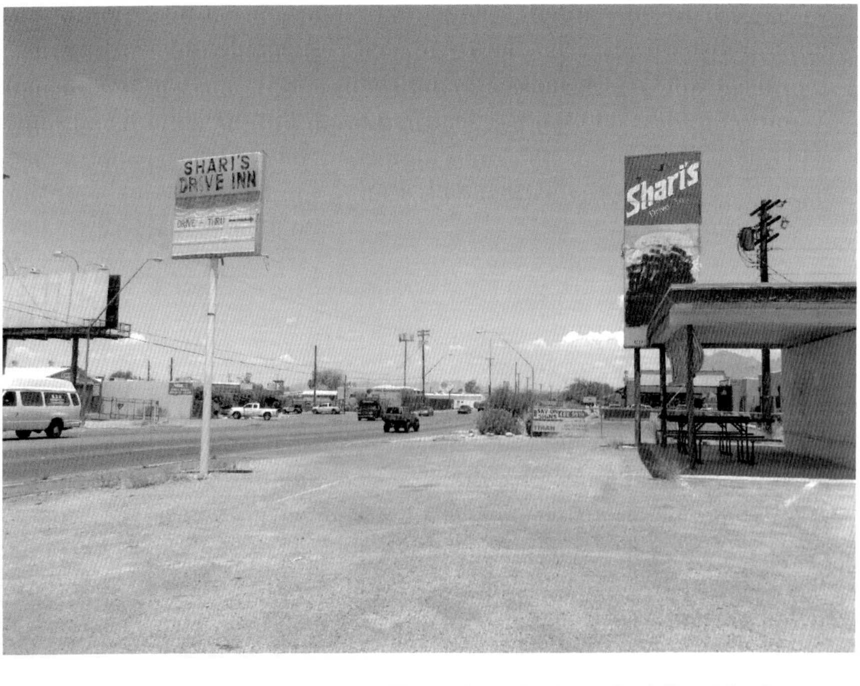

This is how Shari's looks today—very different from the days of a full parking lot. *Author's collection.*

cream was used, and flavors included coffee, pineapple and peanut butter. Other menu items included hot dogs from the grill and chicken.

You ordered through the drive-up window or out front, where often a couple of red picnic tables were secured to the ground. The window allowed you to see into the kitchen, but it was also covered with sheets of paper with pithy sayings on them. You got a meal and a little bit of philosophy every time you ate there.

In 2007, a young couple bought the business but not the building from Joseph Giuffre. They admitted that purchasing Shari's was strictly an investment and that perhaps their hearts weren't in the business.[172] Today, the building stands empty, a little more worn and tired looking—a sad tribute to a great little neighborhood burger joint.

Tastes of Home

Frampton-Stone Cafeteria

Margaret Stone and Reatha Frampton ran this Tucson institution for more than fifty years. They were both from Pennsylvania and were in their fifties when they opened the business on Fourth Avenue in 1949.[173] With reasonable prices, Frampton-Stone attracted a solid group of seniors and hundreds of starving students alike. On certain Friday nights, there was a piano player, although for this writer, Sunday dinner was the time to dine at Frampton-Stone.

The menu featured the kinds of food mom used to make: roast turkey with all the trimmings, carved roast beef with mashed potatoes and gravy, fried chicken so good you'd swear your granny was in the kitchen, meatloaf, baked ham, homemade bread, dumplings, an assortment of salads and desserts that rivaled any found at the county fair.

The kitchen was run under the capable hands of Don Swartz, a chef with Pennsylvania Dutch roots. He brought his heritage to everything he cooked. Swartz worked there for thirty years.[174] Out front, customers would grab a tray and tell the women behind the line what they wanted. Portions were generous, and all the ladies could've been your favorite aunt or that lady from your high school cafeteria. Only coffee, tea or milk was offered, so one didn't even think about asking for a soda with dinner.

Charles Kendrick, of the original Mr. K's BBQ, remembered that Frampton-Stone was probably the second restaurant in town that served

African Americans in the early 1950s.[175] Stone and Frampton ran the place until 1977 and then sold it to Michael Eggers. He closed the place in February 1981. Later that year, Margaret bought the place back and then sold it to David and Gail Sutter. The Sutters ran it for two more years.

Smoke Gets in Your Eyes

In 1998, the City of Tucson enacted a strict smoking law that affected small businesses, especially restaurants. Civic code11-199(E) (2) prohibited "restaurant owners from allowing persons to smoke except in designated areas." Many restaurant owners, especially those of smaller places that didn't have bars or patios, felt that they were being unfairly targeted. Letters to the editor were filled with angry opinions for weeks (from both sides, it must be noted).

Molly Grezaffi, owner of Molly G's on Fort Lowell Road, found a loophole in the law whereby smoking was allowed in private dining clubs. So Molly G's regulars, those who smoked at least, could pay one dollar a year for the privilege of smoking while they enjoyed their eggs over easy or a chicken fried steak. Still, the city cited Grezaffi. She appealed the citation twice but was denied, according to the details in *City of Tucson v. Molly Grezaffi*. Molly G's eventually closed. Whether the legal hassles had anything to do with the closure is up for debate.

Later in 2007, the state created Proposition 201, which stated, "Smoking is not allowed in most enclosed public places of employment including: restaurants, bars, grocery stores or an establishment that serves food." This ruling did seem to have serious repercussions in the hospitality industry. John Condiss, who owned the Olive Tree Greek restaurant for thirty years, estimated that he lost $15,000 in yearly revenue. He cited that loss as one of the reasons he closed his restaurant in 2008. Was Condiss overstating the issue? Perhaps not, as in 2008 more than forty-four other restaurants closed in Tucson alone, the highest number of closures from any previous year or for many years to follow, according to the *Tucson Citizen* archives.

Austin's Old-Fashioned Ice Cream

Old-fashioned was a good thing at Austin's. It meant ice cream made in house; thick shakes served in the icy-cold containers they were made in;[176] big juicy burgers; and friendly, everyone-knows-your-name service.

Eleanor and Merrill Austin opened their ice cream shop in 1959 in the very chic Broadway Village Shopping Center. The center had been designed by Josiah Joseler, who became Tucson's most famous architect.[177] Austin's was the place to go for many years. Families would feel comfortable sitting next to a booth packed with "rowdy" teenagers. Diners, sitting at the large counter, could watch their food being made on the griddle.[178] There were no TVs, and Austin's didn't accept credit cards.

And while ice cream treats (the sundaes were legendary) were the most popular items on the menu, Austin's put out other great food. The hot dog came with mustard, relish, onions and cheese. If you wanted sauerkraut or chili, it would cost a little more. The barbecue beef sandwich was popular, and the chicken salad sandwich held tiny chunks of white meat with just the right amount of mayonnaise. All the sodas were made from syrup and soda water.

The Austins sold the shop in 1985 to Mike Moran, who tried to keep the spirit of an old-fashioned ice cream parlor alive. He used the same equipment and the same recipes for all that delicious ice cream. Even the linoleum lasted until Austin's moved farther east in 2006.[179] By that time, there were other owners who were trying to re-create that sense of old-fashioned goodness, but Austin's Old-Fashioned Ice Cream never was the same. The doors closed in 2009.[180]

The Crying Onion

In the 1970s, the Crying Onion was a funky little café that catered to late-night diners on their way home from the bars. The huge omelets and Texas toast worked their magic, and people could leave the Crying Onion a little more sober and sated. Other items on the menu included stuffed squid, fried smelt in curry sauce and other Mediterranean specialties.

The Crying Onion was in a former farmhouse, and when the new owner, Homer Pappageorge, decided to do some redecorating, he made an interesting discovery. As he began tearing up the beat-up linoleum, he found numerous old newspapers dating as far back as 1880s. Rather than throwing his find in the trash, Pappageorge made a collage on one of the walls. It served as entertainment for many years after that.[181]

Not all customers rolled in at wee hours. During the day, the Crying Onion had a regular customer base. One such regular was known only as "Mr. Jim." Mr. Jim ate there every day. But then, after one $5 meal, Mr. Jim left a tip of $100 and, quite mysteriously, never returned.[182]

Arroyo Café and the Good Earth

Two restaurants fed generations of Tucsonans, and although they were different in style and substance, these two cafés had a commitment to serving good food and making their customers happy.

The first is the Arroyo Café, which operated on Speedway Boulevard at the Arcadia wash (*arroyo* is the Spanish word for creek/wash). First opened in 1946 by a woman named Margaret Meadows and later owned by Herman and Marjorie Erbert, the Arroyo served breakfast, lunch and dinner in typical diner fashion. That meant from-scratch meals, hand-crafted pies and lots and lots of coffee.[183]

Items on the menu included liver and onions, short ribs, stuffed pork chops, meatloaf, mashed potatoes, vegetables, rolls and pies—glorious, glorious pies. Those pies were made fresh every morning. One fan remembered the peanut butter pie as being his go-to choice.[184] We're not sure when it closed, but today the building still houses a restaurant called Oregano's, a pizza chain out of Phoenix.

The Good Earth, which opened in 1968, was just up the road on Speedway Boulevard and Wilmot Road. The focus here was on healthy foods, but that didn't mean that things were bland or heavy. Like at the Arroyo, much of the food was made in house including breads and pies (and a whole host of other baked goods).

Owner Norm Land took the ordinary, not-so-healthy diner food and turned it into something crave-worthy and good for you. The Good Earth Burrito is a prime example. Instead of lard-cooked refried beans, the burrito was stuffed with adzuki beans and seasoned extra-lean ground beef wrapped in a whole wheat chapati. It was then topped with house-made guacamole, sour cream, tomatoes, lettuce and cheeses.[185] There was also always a quiche of the day, several homemade soups and a fish of the day.

In 1986, the Good Earth closed, due in part to some issues with the franchise of the same name. About a year and a half later, Land reopened it under the name Terra Nova with a similar menu.[186] It didn't have a long life.

The Grill

From an interview with Frank Powers and Karlen Ross, June 2015.

Either people "got" the Grill or they didn't. This twenty-four-hour diner had in the 1930s been the home to the Minerva Café.[187] It opened as the Grill in 1994 and, in 1999, was purchased by Patrick and Laurie Forysthe.

The Minerva served as the heart of the Greek community in town. For a while, it was the Stag Grill and then the Rallis Grill, where businessmen rubbed elbows with teenagers skipping school. But the Minerva was the place where you could spend time with other transplants, keep up with the news from home, have a good meal and share a sense of place. The Grill served much the same purpose. The vibe was a little edgier and the food was all-American diner fare, but the Grill attracted people who shared the same outlook on life. It was like family, and even today many of the employees are friends.

The busiest hours were after the bars closed, and so the clientele was often drunk and could get a little rowdy. Often there were only two servers

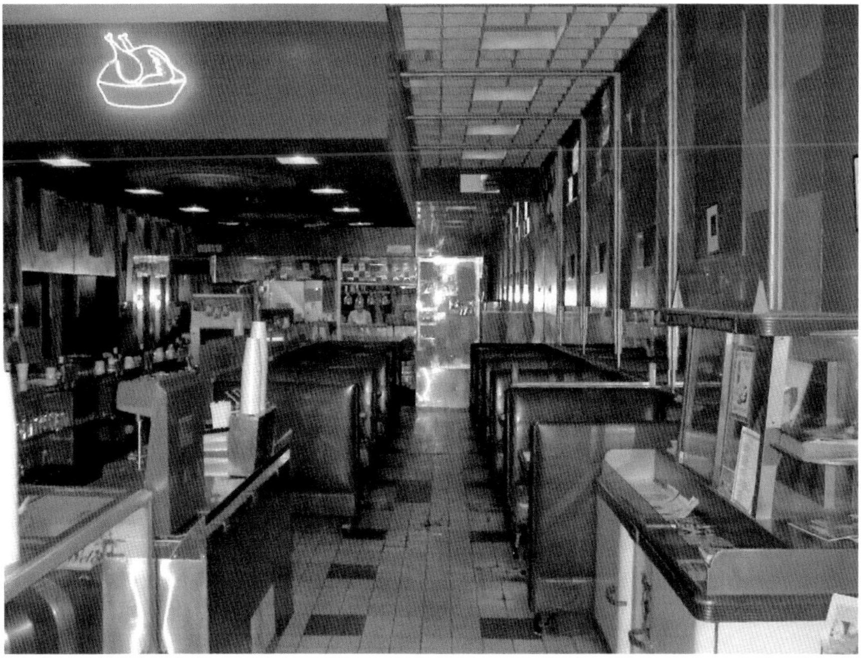

Interior view of the Grill. *Photo by Frank Powers.*

to handle the large group that stumbled in all at once at around 1:00 a.m. Downtown wasn't the trendy area it is these days, and if the police had to be called, the response could take forty-five minutes or more. The staff handled the situation with a large dose of we-don't-care-sit-down-and-eat-your-food attitude.

In fact, the menu had a long "manifesto" that explained why things were done the way they were and what was expected from the diners. That attitude was part of the charm of the Grill, and according to Frank Powers, who worked there for about five years, most of the customers understood. Other rules included no ranch dressing, no artificial sweeteners, no American cheese and—whatever you do—no ordering of cheese on the tater tots. In fact, that tots rule was part of the contract in the building, according to Powers. Some people didn't appreciate the sass, but the Grill was a perennial winner of "Best of Tucson—Late Night Eats" and "Best Diner," so it was obviously doing something right.

The kitchen had a lot of latitude when it came to creating the cuisine. Nothing came from a can. Powders and packaged mixes were never used. The chefs were adamant about that rule. The tots were perhaps the most memorable menu item, but the Grill also served made-from-scratch soups, salads with freshly made house dressings, pastas from the local Italian deli, steaks, burgers, sandwiches and, of course, breakfast. There was only one appetizer, the fried ravioli. Called "Death Bombs" or "DB's," these were one of the most popular items on the menu. At least six pasta dishes were served, three of which were tortellini. The Freaking Great Tortellini consisted of pasta topped with fresh spinach, chives and a creamy garlic and parmesan sauce. It was a big seller, especially late at night.

The space was divided into two areas. The main dining room held a long, semicircular counter and red vinyl booths that could accommodate a large party. Large picture windows allowed for great people watching on Congress. The adjacent Red Room was built to fit the nighttime crowd. There was a piano (that only certain people were allowed to play) and space to accommodate the live music that was part of the scene. Bands traveling through town would pop in for impromptu sessions and play for ham sandwiches and a few beers.

In 2008, Forsythe called a handful of the employees, including Karlen Ross, into the office and told them basically that either he could close the Grill at the end of the month or they could become partial owners because he was joining the navy. Because the Grill was so important to them, they accepted the offer, and each owned 10 percent for a number of years. Finally, though,

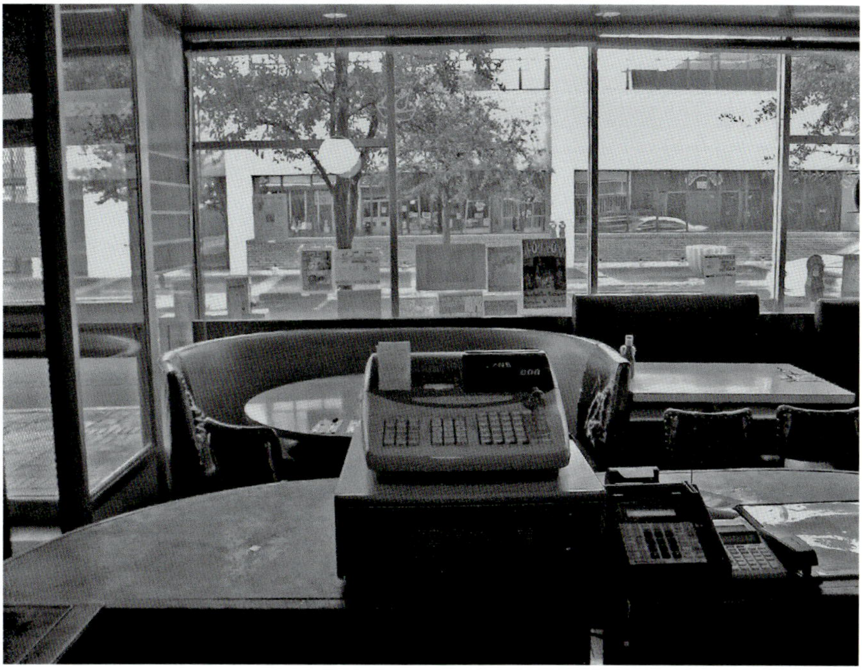

Standing in the Grill and looking out to Congress Street. *Photo by Frank Powers.*

a decision was made to close permanently, and the Grill shut the doors in November 2011. A sign on the door read "Open Never," and that was that. Then, in the early morning hours of January 1, 2013, a fire scorched the building. That was pretty much it for this iconic counter-culture diner.

University Eats

When Tucson lost being named the territorial capital to Prescott, city leaders weren't happy in the least. Getting the state university wasn't much of a consolation prize either as far as they were concerned, so they chose to locate the campus as far away from the center of town as possible. Through a donation by several gamblers, a tract of land four miles from the heart of the city was designated for the campus.

Construction began on the building now known as Old Main, and by 1891, the first classes were being held. Total enrollment was thirty-two students, with a staff of six teachers.[188] By 1924, the university was as much a

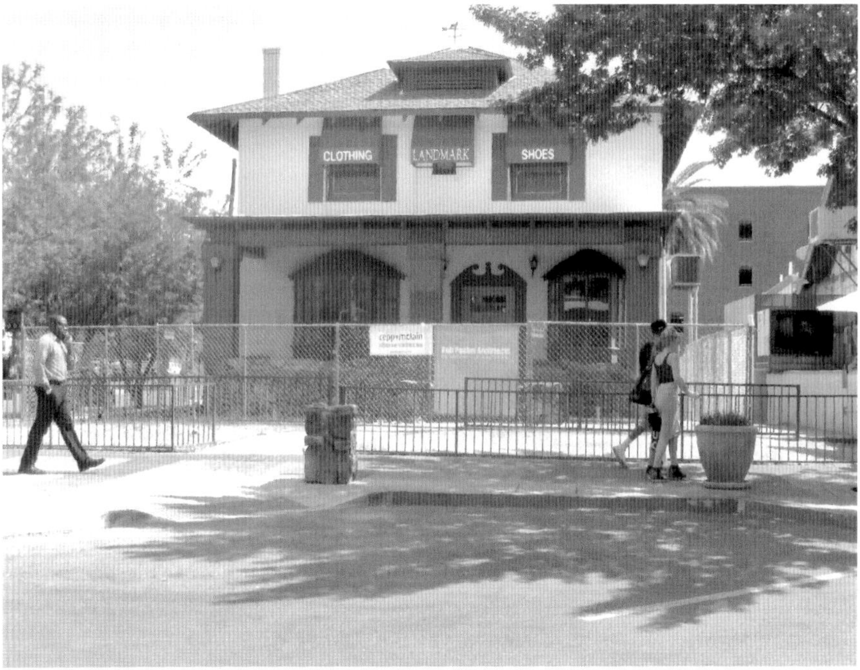

This old house was the home of the Varsity Inn, a college hangout for decades. *Author's collection.*

part of the city as gambling had ever been. Businesses, even some restaurants, sprang up. The Marshall family owned a substantial tract of land just west of campus, and they wisely created the Marshall Square, which even today, under the name Main Gate Square, serves as major retail area for the college crowd.

The area had three very popular restaurants: the Copper Kettle, the Yucca Tea Room and the Varsity Inn. The Varsity, which was in a converted house, helped put a lot of people through college. It lasted through the late 1960s but had by that time become a "greasy spoon," according to Dr. Jim Griffith, a former University of Arizona professor and Tucson's most famous folklorist. He recalled eating many a bologna sandwich there. It later became the site of Franklin's Men's Wear.[189]

The Yucca Tea Room had also been a private home. Over the decades, the building also was used as an inn and a fraternity house. Then, in 1961, a group purchased the building and turned it into Gentle Ben's, an extremely popular college bar.[190] The building was torn down, and Gentle Ben's moved up the block. A Marriot Hotel, which serves university visitors, now sits on the site.

The Big A

If you were making a movie about college life in the 1960s and '70s and needed an inspiration for a hangout, you couldn't find a better place than the Big A, located on Speedway Boulevard at Campbell Avenue, which was as close to the University of Arizona's campus as you could get without actually being on campus. The building abutted the sidewalk (which later would affect the Big A in a negative way). The sign, a single block letter *A*, could be seen for blocks. Geraniums hung from window boxes out front, which was a bit misleading, as once you got inside, the décor was all collegiate, all the time.

The walls were dark wood paneling. The wooden booths were deep and scarred with customer's initials. Pennants from both the U of A and rivals were hung jauntily on the walls. And there was the Coaches Corner, a special table reserved for any coach who might show up.

You ordered at the counter from a menu that hung on a wall behind that counter. The Big A served a mix of items, but people went there for burgers—big, juicy, broiled burgers. They were all numbered; maybe there were ten in all, if you counted the number 6½. Everyone had their favorite—the mushroom burger, the blue cheese burger with a thick slice of tomato or the cheeseburger made with real English cheddar. Drinks were all served in mason jars. You couldn't get a beer until 1966, about five years after it had opened. There were a few desserts, the most famous being a chocolate fudge pie.

The Big A was a popular spot on game days; it was an easy walk to either the football field or basketball stadium from there, but on any given night, you could find students, professors or neighbors enjoying well-made burgers and baskets of onion rings.

The original owners were Pete and Martha Petersen, who ran the place until 1979, which is when Rosemary and Bill Seery took over.[191] The Seerys knew that they had good thing going and didn't change an inch of the place. But in 1987, the city decided that it was time to widen Speedway, and because the Big A was so close to the street front, it had to be destroyed. The owner of the building (not the Seerys) opted to keep the back portion, and the Seerys were forced to either close or move. It took two years for the widening project to get started (the restaurant remained open throughout that whole time), but in 1989, the Seerys found a site two blocks away and across the street. They moved everything—lock, stock and Coaches Corner—to the new site.[192]

Rosemary died in 1997 and Bill was in frail health, so son Brian took over managing the restaurant. Brian sold the business to Gene Fuller in 1998.[193] A year later, the Big A closed for good.

The Bum Steer

From an interview with Matt Russell, July 2015.

The Bum Steer had two distinct personalities. By day it was a fun family place where people gathered to eat and gaze at the amazing amalgamation of stuff hanging from the walls. The building was a split-level three-story monstrosity and was filled to the rafters with deer heads, movie posters, license plates, farm tools, knickknacks and even an airplane. No matter where one sat, the views were entertaining. There were peanut shells on the floor, the music was kept at a decent level and the menu had something for everyone. It was fun to send someone who had never been there before to the bathrooms, where the signs for the men's and women's rooms were conveniently interchanged. People would wait and watch to see how long it took for the victim to discover the mistake.

By night, it was, for a time, one of the highest-volume college bars and restaurants around. Every night at 8:00 p.m., the announcement would go out: "Ladies and gentlemen, welcome to the world famous Bum Steer, where there is never a cover charge. It is now time for anyone under twenty-one years of age to leave the bar." It was not unusual on weekend evenings to see a line of people waiting to get in literally wrapped around the building. Wednesday evenings were the same, thanks to the special "White Wednesdays," where all white liquor drinks were insanely priced at seventy-nine cents. There were two bars on each of the three levels, and the bartenders were kept busy.

Daytime would find the place filled with a low-key mix of folks. Kids could play on the pinball machines and video games (*Pac-Man* was quite popular). College kids could bring their visiting parents there, assuring them that the place where their children hung out was safe and clean.

In the kitchen, all the food was made from scratch. Fresh mushrooms and zucchini were cut and dipped in an egg wash and tossed with the house breading before being deep fried. The Steer was one of the first places to serve chicken wings, which were served with the house-made blue cheese dressing. Fresh ground beef was used in the burgers.

Matt Russell of Russell Communications and host of *On the Menu Live…with Matt Russell*, a local foodie radio show, worked at the Bum Steer starting as a line cook in 1987. "The thing I like most about the Bum Steer, and I think it is authentic to say, is that the Bum Steer was one of the first restaurants to play creatively with what a burger is about."

The basic Steer Burger was good, but Russell said there were at least eight or ten others, including the Bravo Avo, which was topped with pepper jack cheese, avocado, sour cream and green chiles. And then there was the Jiffy Burger, which included jack cheese, bacon and peanut butter. "At first glance, you'd say there's no way this is edible," he said, "and then once you began to see the heat of the burger begin to melt the peanut butter as it cascaded over the burger…beautiful!"

Russell also described the Mental Onion Block, a bumped-up take on onion rings. Fresh onions were sliced, dipped in buttermilk and a coating and then fried in deep fryer basket. The buttermilk and coating would "cement" together, creating a solid block of onions that would be popped out of the basket piping hot. Peanuts were kept in a hopper on the third floor, and when people on the lower floors opened a small door, the peanuts would slide down a chute into the person's paper basket.

Once night fell, the students took over. There was dancing on the third level. It could get rowdy, but for the most part, the Steer was a fun place to hang. Russell, by this time, got called up to be a bartender. He has many stories to tell, but he noted that the owners (Grand American Fare) treated the staff well, feeding them for free on the days they worked, providing a study space for the many U of A kids who worked there and paying fifty dollars if you got hit trying to break up a fight. He also noted that he met his wife, Nancy, there. Russell left in 1989, but during his time at the Bum Steer, the owner built sand volleyball courts outside in the parking lot, which added a whole other element to the fun at the Steer.

Owners changed, and so did the crowd. Almost overnight the Bum Steer developed a reputation as a not-so-safe place to be. The police were called to break up disturbances on a regular basis. In 2005, a man was shot and killed in the parking lot. Politics, misunderstanding of the complicated liquor laws and a reluctance on the part of the city police to recommend a renewal led to an eventual closure.

In 2007, another set of owners attempted to get a liquor license. They'd spent thousands of dollars in renovations in an attempt to return the Bum Steer into a family restaurant.[194] In a city council meeting to get a recommendation for renewal, people came forward with stories about the

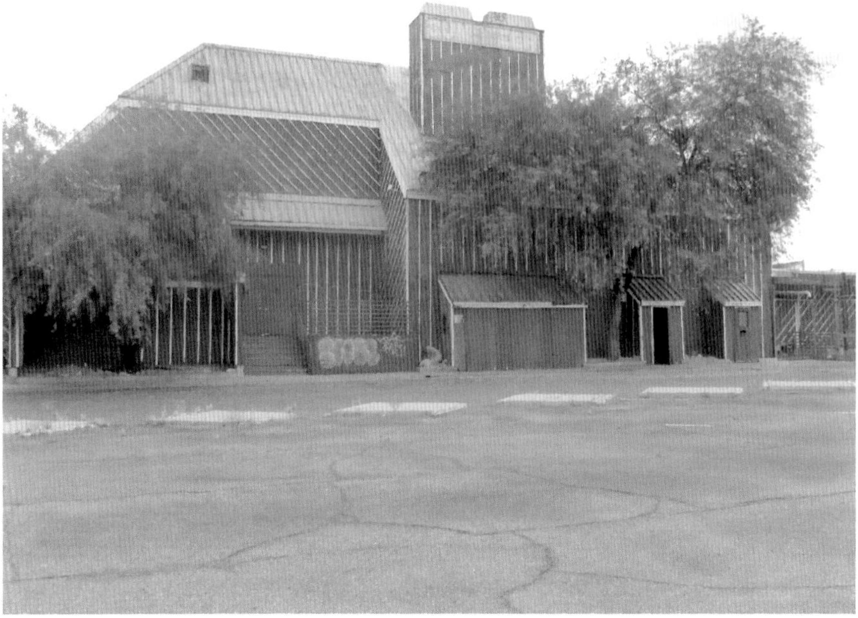

The Bum Steer today. On weekend nights, the line to get in would wrap around the building. *Author's collection.*

beloved restaurant. A story was told by the owner about woman coming in with a box in her hand. In the box were her husband's ashes.[195] She told them how happy she was about their efforts and explained that it was the thirtieth anniversary of the day he had proposed to her at the restaurant. Others testified about how the changes were positive ones and how they felt that the Steer was again a family place, a place to build memories.

The city council denied a recommendation, and the state liquor board denied a license because the Steer didn't meet the requirements of food-to-liquor ratio. Today, the building stands empty (except for all the stuff still inside) and is used at Halloween as a haunted house.

The Last Chance Pizza Mill

The Last Chance Pizza Mill introduced deep-dish pizza to Tucson. When it opened on Friday, December 13, 1974, the lines reached out the doors, and it ran out of pizza long before closing time. There was plenty of beer on hand, however, so customers were happy. Located just west of the University of Arizona campus, the Mill was a perfect place to hang after classes and well into the evening.

Friends Steve Marshall, Charlie Langford and Mark "Buzz" Farlow were from Urbana, Illinois, and wanted to bring a little bit of home to Tucson. Their inspiration was Garcia's Pizza, located near the University of Illinois campus in Champagne/Urbana. They hired two women, one who had worked at Garcia's and another who had worked at Pizzeria Uno in Chicago, to help develop the recipe.[196]

There were salads, but the pizza was what brought people in the door. Twelve inches across and two inches thick, the pizzas were topped with the usual items, with the OD having all of the toppings. If you could eat one of these monstrosities in an hour, the pizza was free. Many tried, but few succeeded. In 1976, the OD was named "Best Pizza in Tucson." For a short time, sandwiches were also on the menu, but they never attained the popularity of the pies.

You'd never call the place fancy. Wood paneling, a cement floor, beer signs and a pool table were the only décor. Music was always playing, with whoever was slinging pies getting to choose the tunes.

A second Mill was opened on Fourth Avenue, Tucson's hip shopping/dining/partying mecca. That lasted about two years.[197] The original Last Chance Pizza Mill closed on January 2, 1982, much to the sorrow of friends, fans and employees. It took six more years before another restaurant became the go-to deep-dish pizza place.

Zachary's

Zachary's Pizza opened on the East Sixth Street, on the south side of campus. It, too, was immensely popular with the college crowd for many of the same reasons the Last Chance was: great pizza; cold, cheap beer; and a totally casual atmosphere. Dave Ellis was the owner. Zachary's was first located on the north side of the street, but when the university stretched its long fingers and tore down the entire block, Ellis moved across the street. He continued there until 2012, when several years of economic downturn deeply affected business. Original customers were bringing in their kids and a few longtimers hung on, but it just wasn't enough to keep Zachary's going.[198]

Frankie's

For New York pizza lovers, there was no better place to go than Frankie's Pizza. Sadly, little factual information about the business could be found. We do know that there were two Frankie's restaurants: one in the basement of a building just off Sixth Street by the university and the other on Speedway, next to the Lucky Strike Bowling Alley.

Both served pizzas with perfectly chewy crusts, rich pizza sauce, mozzarella and an assortment of toppings. The toppings weren't exotic—maybe there was pineapple. You could get a whole pie or a slice at a price that fit perfectly with a starving student's budget.

The Loft Theater, an off-campus movie house, sat directly above the campus Frankie's. One person remembered sitting in the darkened theater, watching the art flicks and being enveloped by the aromas drifting up from Frankie's. He couldn't wait for the movie to be over. The midtown spot delivered, and it wasn't unusual for the delivery man to bring a case of beer with pies. Frankie's didn't serve beer, so the driver would just make an extra stop along the way.

As stated, few hard facts on Frankie's could be found, but a fire burned down the building by the campus in 1964. The Loft relocated. No one knows whether Frankie's did. Nor can anyone remember when the Speedway Frankie's finally stopped making its tasty pizzas.

Chapter 7

Full Circle

Why does a restaurant go out of business? People like to blame the economy, yet plenty of restaurants survive hard times. Of course, a lack of business sense often plays a part. Issues with landlords can cause numerous problems, especially when it comes to rent and upkeep. With that point, the fault can lie with either party. The rent gets raised; the rent doesn't get paid. The landlord doesn't make required improvements; the renter destroys property. The list goes on and on.

Another common cause is business partners go in different directions or lose sight of the shared passion. And then there's the family. Squabbles and sibling rivalry can play a part. Sadly, sometimes the third or fourth generation just doesn't want all the headaches and hard work that their parents and grandparents accepted as part of the job. Even when they pick up the torch, the passion just isn't there. Sometimes it's just time to close the doors.

In the first half of 2015, more than fifteen restaurants shuttered in Tucson. There were a few chains that moved out of town and a handful of places that really had no chance of success from the onset. But three popular and classic restaurants need to be mentioned.

Bluefin

Sister restaurant to the long-popular Kingfisher, Bluefin was known for great seafood and an old-time clubby feel. It was located in the former Coat of Arms restaurant in Casas Adobe Plaza. Owners Jim Murphy and Jeff Azersky had retained the clubby feel of the place while serving modern food and drink and had a huge following. A summertime special included a full lobster dinner for whatever the year was—you'd get a whole lobster, rice, corn on the cob and drawn butter for $20.13 in 2013. You could always count on an assortment of oysters as well and great wines that paired well with all the menu items.

In late 2014, new owners purchased the plaza. When it was time to renew the lease, the parties involved couldn't come to an agreement. As a matter of respect for their staff, Murphy and Azersky let everyone know about the closure nearly two months ahead of time. It is a testimony to the pair that apart from a few busboys, everyone stuck with them until the last day.[199]

This one will be sorely missed, but fans have faith in the pair. After all, they've been cooking in Tucson since the 1980s. A new venture is, no doubt, just around the corner.

The Dish

The Dish started out as one of those "wouldn't it be fun" ideas among a group of friends. Tom Smith, Jennifer Elchuck, Doug Levy and his future wife, Laura, wanted to open a place that served just side dishes.

By the time it opened, Levy was in the kitchen, Laura was running the front of the house (which was in the Rum Runner, a well-established wine shop) and Tom and Jennifer were owners. With only about forty seats, the menu had also evolved into something a little more. Over time, Doug and Laura left to open their own businesses (Doug opened Feast, which is still going strong). In 2007, the business moved to new building.[200] The menu changed quarterly, but the signature mussels in white wine stayed on the menu. That dish was so iconic that Rachel Ray featured it on her *$40 a Day* show on the Food Network.

Sometime in 2014, Chef Mike Muthart left to grow his chicken ranch in nearby Benson, and Smith began to feel the need for a change.[201] The last dinner at the Dish took place in early 2015.

La Fuente

La Fuente, which means "the Fountain," became the victim of a sinking economy. The year 2008 was an especially hard one for small businesses in Tucson, certainly for restaurants. It was the last holdout on Miracle Mile, closing its doors in late 2014. (It had filed for bankruptcy in 2011.)[202]

Decked out in bright colors with a full assortment of Mexican curios and knickknacks, La Fuente was the kind of place you brought visitors to for a taste and feel of Mexico. Live mariachi music was a big part of the experience. Sunday brunch was an extravaganza. It wasn't uncommon to see a tourist bus in the parking lot

La Fuente was run by the Davis-Huerta family for most of its existence (it opened in 1959). They sold the restaurant to Carlos and Mary Jane Portillo. The Portillos kept the legend of La Fuente alive for ten years. But like many other restaurants in the first part of the new millennium, La Fuente suffered from a bad economy and changing tastes.

Looking Forward

As sad as it was to see these favorites close, Tucson is undergoing a culinary renaissance of sorts. Restaurants of all types, from Native American to Indian to hamburger stands, are opening at a fast clip. The downtown area is booming with new restaurants, among them a spot from award-winning chef Chris Bianco's Bianco's Pizza in Phoenix. Several restaurant owners in town are planning new ventures. Food trucks have moved in and can be found parked all over town.

Some comfort can be taken in the fact that many chefs who worked at the lost restaurants in this book now have other venues. Doug Levy of Terra Cotta and Boccata runs Feast. Janos Wilder welcomes guests old and new at his Downtown Kitchen and Cocktails. Donna Nordin gives cooking classes several times a year. Danny Scordato still has family recipes on the menu at Vivace. The Ali family has two places: Cosmo's daughter Pina's restaurant, Trattoria Pina, and the Damiano family's Michaelangelo's. Joe Abi-Ad runs Joe's Pancake House. Jim Murphy, Jeff Azersky and Marianne Baines continue to serve fantastic meals in a great atmosphere at Kingfisher. And Maria LaMadrid who used to be

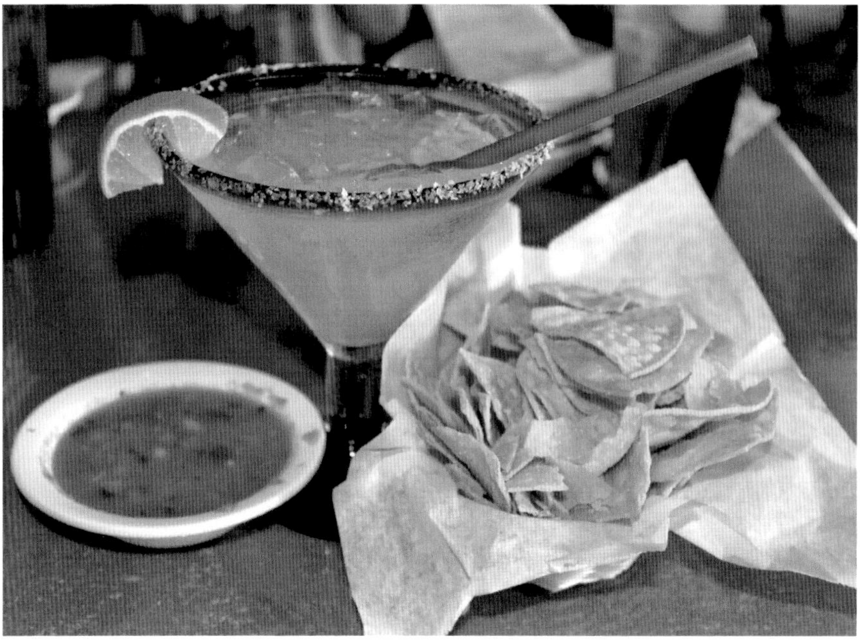

Have a margarita! *Creative Commons.*

married to Bryan Mazon of Papagayo, makes killer tacos at Boca Tacos and Tequila.

Tucson's restaurant scene is alive and well, due in part to the long history of wonderful places to dine.

Notes

Chapter 1

1. City of Tucson, "A Brief History of Tucson," https://www.tucsonaz.gov/info/brief-history-tucson.
2. Estelle M. Buehman, Old Tucson: A Hop, Skip and Jump History from 1539 Indian Settlement to New and Greater Tucson (N.p.: Nebu Press, 1923).
3. New Advent, http://www.newadvent.org.
4. Chris Howell and Rita Connelly, *The Insider's Guide to Tucson*, 2nd ed. (Helena, MT: Falcon Publishing Inc., 2000).
5. City of Tucson, "Brief History of Tucson."
6. Interview with Danny Lee, July 2015.
7. University of Arizona, "In the Steps of Esteban: Tucson's African American History," exhibit, "Through Our Parents' Eyes: History & Culture of Southern Arizona," http://parentseyes.arizona.edu/esteban/photoexhibits.html.
8. Neil Carmody, ed., *Whiskey, Six-Guns and Red Light Ladies: George Hand's Saloon Diaries, 1875–1878* (N.p.: High Lonesome Books, 1995).
9. James E. Officer, "Barriers to Mexican Integration in Tucson," *Kiva* 17, no. 1–2 (November–December 1951): 7–16, http://www.jstor.org/stable/30247072.
10. James Walter Yancy, "The Negro in Tucson: Past and Present," master's thesis, University of Arizona, 1933.
11. Ibid.; Carmody, *Whiskey, Six-Guns and Red Light Ladies*.
12. Grace Peña Delgado, "Of Kith and Kin: Land, Leases and Guanxi in Tucson's Chinese and Mexican Communities 1880s—1920s," *Journal of Arizona History* (Spring 2005).

13. Ibid.
14. *Arizona Daily Star*, June 15, 1969.
15. Alex Jay Kimmelman, "Strictly White and Always Sober: Tucson's Pioneer Hotels: A Photo Essay," *Journal of Arizona History* 35, no. 1 (Spring 1994): 63–80, http://www.jstor.org/stable/41696066.
16. Audrey Hunter, "Shoo Fly Restaurant Famed and Defamed," *Arizona Daily Star*, September 21, 1958.
17. Interview with Bryan and Alice Mazon, June 2015.
18. Alex Levin, "Tucson Fire Department," 2nd edition, Tucson Fire Foundation, www.tucsonfirefoundation.com/2012/07/levin-Alexander-2nd-ed-pdf.
19. Carmody, *Whiskey, Six-Guns and Red Light Ladies*.
20. Ibid.
21. *Arizona Citizen*, April 4, 1879.
22. Ibid., April 10, 1880.
23. Howell and Connelly, *Insider's Guide to Tucson*.
24. Downtown Tucson Partnership, http://www.downtowntucson.org.
25. *Arizona Business Directory and Gazetteer* (San Francisco, CA: W.C. Disturnell, 1881).
26. Rochester Ford, "Tucson, Arizona" *Out West* 17, no 1–3 (September 1902).
27. Patricia Stephenson, "Tom Marshall's Tucson," "Through Our Parents' Eyes."
28. Interview with Dr. James Griffith, June 2015.
29. Yancy, "Negroes in Tucson."
30. University of Arizona, "In the Steps of Esteban."
31. Interview with Mr. Charles Kendrick, July 2015.
32. Tiffany Kjos, *Arizona Daily Star*, "George Miller, Tucson Mayor in 1990s, Dies," http://tucson.com/news/local/george-miller-tucson-mayor-in-s-dies/article_dc9bc76c-cb5e-57c9-a0ae-35653c213ac3.html.
33. Demion Clinco, *Historic Miracle Mile Tucson's Northern Auto Gateway: A Historic Context Study for the Oracle Area*, prepared for the City of Tucson's Historic Preservation Office, Department of Urban Planning and Design, 2009.
34. City of Tucson, "Brief History of Tucson."
35. Interview with James Murphy, Jeff Azersky and Marianne Baines, July 2015; interview with Jonathan Landeen, June 2015.
36. Rita Connelly, "Indie Inspirations," *Tucson Weekly*, February 9, 2006; interviews with Don Luria, January 2006 and July 2015.

Chapter 2

37. Carmody, *Whiskey, Six-Guns and Red Light Ladies.*
38. Interview with Bryan and Alice Mazon, June 2015.
39. Bob Rhodes, "Tea Room Has Housed Troops of Mexico: Remnants of Walls of Old Pueblo Seen in Patio," *Tucson Citizen*, March 20, 1928.
40. Susan Myal, *Tucson's Mexican Restaurants: Repast, Recipes and Remembrances* (Tucson: University of Arizona Press, 1999).
41. *Arizona Daily Star*, Yndia Smalley Moore obituary.
42. Interview with Bryan and Alice Mezon, June 2015.
43. Michele Keating, "Pancho's from Rags to Riches," *Tucson Citizen*, January 18, 1968.
44. Ibid.
45. Interview with Frank Gonzales III, July 2015.
46. Lindi Laws, John Long and Tuppi Long, eds. and comps., *Menus of Tucson's Finest Restaurants* (N.p.: Quail Run Publications, 1980); Pancho's menu.
47. Interview with Frank Gonzales III, July 2015.
48. Ibid.
49. Interview with Michelle Araneta and Ginger and Michael Master, July 2015.
50. Mexico Inn menu.
51. Kathleen Allen, "Mexico Inn, Survivor and Benefactor to Close," *Tucson Citizen*, December 6, 1990.
52. Interview with Michelle Araneta and Ginger and Michael Master, July 2015.
53. Ibid.
54. Ed Severson, "Don't Bother the Cook," *Arizona Daily Star*, June 26, 1980.
55. Rita Connelly, "A Pinch of Prickly Pear," TucsonWeekly.com, March 8, 2012, comments section.
56. Interview with Marguerite Brown and Julie Valenzuela, June 2015.
57. Ibid.
58. Ibid.
59. Carlotta Flores, *El Charro Café: The Tastes and Traditions of Tucson* (Tucson, AZ: Fisher Books, 1998).
60. Ed Lopez, "El Chapparal to Vanish from DeGrazia's Old Campbell Avenue Home," *Arizona Daily Star*, January 8, 1983.
61. Interview Bryan and Alice Mezon, June 2015.
62. Ibid.
63. Ibid.
64. Old Adobe menu, Arizona Historical Society.
65. Kathy Burns, "Adios El Adobe," *Tucson Weekly*, October 16, 1994.

Chapter 3

66. Rita Connelly, "Hidden Valley Haven," *Tucson Weekly*, March 2005.
67. Hidden Valley menu, 2005.
68. Jon Burnstein, "Kitchen Fire Guts Hidden Valley Inn," *Tucson Citizen*, August 8, 1995.
69. Charlotte O. Valdez, "Hidden Valley Carvings Spared," *Tucson Citizen*, August 9, 1995.
70. Interview with Jimmy Gekas, July 2015.
71. Chris Limberis, "Here's the Beef," *Tucson Weekly*, February 25, 2003.
72. *Triple C Chuckwagon*, pamphlet, Arizona Historical Society.

Chapter 4

73. *Tucson Citizen*, "Rossi's, Beloved of Every Tucson Old-Timer, Will Pass from View within Fortnight," May 1920.
74. Paul L. Allen, "Rossi's Was The Place to Eat," *Tucson Citizen*, May 2, 2005.
75. Rossi's menu, circa 1918.
76. Allen, "Rossi's Was The Place to Eat."
77. Rossi's menu, circa 1918.
78. Allen, "Rossi's Was The Place to Eat."
79. Rhonda Bodfield Bloom, "Mary, Full of Grace," *Arizona Daily Star*, February 6, 2005.
80. Interview with Kiki Kinkade, James Gekas and Genie Patterson, June 2015.
81. Promotional pamphlet for Sirloin & Saddle.
82. Interview with Kiki Kinkade, James Gekas and Genie Patterson, June 2015.
83. Ibid.
84. Ibid.
85. Interview with Chuck Hamm, June 2015.
86. Interview with Kiki Kinkade, James Gekas and Genie Patterson, June 2015.
87. Bloom, "Mary, Full of Grace."
88. Ibid.
89. Interview with Douglas and Rita Marvin, June 2004.
90. Rita Connelly, "Sorely Missed," *Tucson Weekly*, October 10, 2008.
91. Iron Mask menu.
92. Clinco, *Historic Miracle Mile*.
93. Bonnie Henry, "Former Barbecue Stand Has Become a Tucson Landmark," *Arizona Daily Star*, August 5, 1987.
94. *Arizona Daily Star*, Dean Short obituary, July 2015.
95. Critiki—Guide to Tiki Bars and Polynesian Restaurants, http://critiki.com.

96. Ibid.

97. Interview with Daniel Scordato, January 2008.

98. Ibid., July 2015.

99. Ibid., January 2008.

100. Ibid., January 2008 and July 2015; interview with Joseph Scordato, January 2005.

101. A.J. Flick, "Scordato Must Pay for Using His Name," *Tucson Citizen*, July 29, 2004.

102. Interview with Daniel Scordato, July 2015.

103. Interview with Michael Veres, June 2015.

104. Interview with Jonathan Landeen, July 2015.

105. Ibid.

106. Janos Wilder, *Janos: Recipes & Tales from a Southwest Kitchen* (N.p.: Ten Speed Press, 1989).

107. Tom Pew and Laurie Pew, "Janos: A Modern Menu in an Old House," *Tucson Citizen*, 1984.

108. Interview with Doug Levy, June 2015.

109. Interview with Jeff Azursky, July 2015.

110. Interview with Marianne Baines, July 2015.

111. Interview with Alan Zeman, July 2015.

112. Ibid.

113. Ibid.

114. Interview with Ryan Clark, June 2015.

115. Interview with Alan Zeman, July 2015.

116. Interview with Ellen Burke Van Slyke, June 2015.

117. Ibid Interview with Ellen Burke Van Slyke, June 2015.

118. Ibid.

119. Interview with Jonathan Landeen, June 2015.

120. Interview with Jim "Murph" Murphy, Jeff Azersky and Marianne Baines, July 2015.

121. Karen S. Gerdron, *The Old Pueblo Review: Complete Menu Guide and Reviews of Tucson's Favorite Restaurants and Entertainment* (N.p.: Treasure Chest Publications, 1990).

122. *Tucson Weekly*, "Best of Tucson," 2008.

123. Rebecca Cook, "Nonie Is a Fabulous Fragment of New Orleans Cuisine Heaven," *Tucson Weekly: Bayou Bistro*, http://www.tucsonweekly.com/tw/02-19-98/chow.htm.

124. Anthony's menu.

125. Cathalena E. Burch, "Tucson Loses Anthony's in the Catalinas," *Arizona Daily Star*, September 4, 2013, http://tucson.com/entertainment/dining/restaurants/tucson-loses-anthony-s-in-the-catalinas/article_40ebee4c-ee25-5003-aa5d-40827ea091ac.html.

126. Ibid.

Chapter 5

127. Interview with Vince and Assunta Ali, July 2015.
128. Rita Connelly, "Italian Style," *Tucson Weekly*, October 28, 2008.
129. Interviews with Pina Colosimo, August 2010 and July 2015.
130. Ibid.
131. Interview with Vince and Assunta Ali, July 2015.
132. Ibid.
133. Ibid.
134. Interview with Tess O'Shea, July 2015.
135. Fiorito's menu.
136. Adam Borowitz, "It's Not Looking Good for Fiorito's," *Tucson Weekly: The Range*, November 3, 2010.
137. Interview with Danny Lee, July 2015.
138. Ibid.
139. Rita Connelly, "Sorely Missed."
140. Interview with Kim Moran, July 2015.
141. Ibid.
142. Ibid.
143. Deborah Block, "Gambling on French Food—and Tucson's Tastes," *Tucson Citizen*, May 16, 1978.
144. Interview with Dr. Patricia Sparks, July 2015.
145. Gerdron, *Old Pueblo Review*.
146. Interview with Dr. Patricia Sparks, July 2015.
147. Interview with Joe Abi-Ad, July 2015.
148. Ibid.
149. Chuck Graham, "El Greco's Folksy Touches Abound," *Tucson Citizen*, March 6, 1997.
150. Interview with Michael "Benny" Benedetto, July 2015.
151. Ibid.
152. Gerdron, *Old Pueblo Review*; the Olive Tree menu.
153. Interview with Michael "Benny" Benedetto, July 2015.
154. *Tucson Citizen* Archives, "Tucson Citizen Morgue, Part 1 (2006–2009)," http://tucsoncitizen.com/morgue.
155. Ernesto Portillo Jr., "Neto's Tucson: Better Order Your Plate of Love Now," *Arizona Daily Star*, May 25, 2008, http://tucson.com/news/local/neto-s-tucson-better-order-your-plate-of-love-now/article_c34265ba-2352-5080-89de-52eceef68a86.html.
156. Ibid.
157. Judy Lefton, "Back in Business," *Tucson Citizen*, January 21, 1988.

158. Ana Terrazas, "Barbecue Trade Suits Lawyer," *Tucson Citizen*, February 14, 1986.
159. Dave Mendez, "Jack's Original Barbecue Is Closing Today," *Tucson Weekly*, August 18, 2012, http://www.tucsonweekly.com/TheRange/archives/2012/08/18/jacks-original-barbecue-is-closing-today.
160. Interview with Mr. Charles Kendrick, July 2015.

Chapter 6

161. Americans for Nonsmokers' Rights, *City of Tucson v. Molly Grezaffi*, http://www.no-smoke.org/pdf/tucsondecision.pdf.
162. Frontier Drive-in menu.
163. African American History Place, "Black History in Arizona," http://www.africanamericanhistoryplace.com/Arizona.html.
164. Interview with Mr. Charles Kendrick, July 2015.
165. Bonnie Henry, "Dixie Drive-in Held Sway in Days Before Freeways," *Arizona Daily Star*, July 5, 1989.
166. Robert Zucker, "Tucson's Culture in Fried Chicken," *Entertainment* 1 (2014), http://entertaintucson.com/volumeone/polarbar.html.
167. Ibid.
168. Lucky Wishbone, "History," http://www.luckywishbone.com/history.html.
169. Various interviews, July 2015.
170. Bonnie Henry, "Johnie's Was the Place to Show Off the Family Wheels, Visit with the Gang," *Arizona Daily Star*, April 1, 1987.
171. Cathalena E. Burch, "Tucson Loses a Favorite as Shari's Closes," *Arizona Daily Star*, http://tucson.com/news/tucson-loses-a-favorite-as-shari-s-closes-down/article_26730159-7fac-5755-8b0b-80ea0ac7376e.html.
172. Ibid.
173. Thomas P. Lee, "Closed Café," *Arizona Daily Star*, July 3, 1981.
174. Ibid.; *Tucson Citizen*, "Cafeteria Stirs Memories," May 27, 1981.
175. Interview with Mr. Charles Kendrik.
176. Jimmy Boegle, "Old Fashioned Eats," *Tucson Weekly*, July 31, 2003.
177. E.L. Sigesmund, "Restaurant Thrives on a Taste of the Past," *Tucson Citizen*, June 10, 1991.
178. Interview with Andrea Davis, July 2015.
179. Sigesmund, "Restaurant Thrives on a Taste of the Past."
180. Adam Borowitz, "Austin's Old Fashioned Ice Cream Apparently Closed," *Tucson Weekly*, December 8, 2009, http://www.tucsonweekly.com/TheRange/archives/2009/12/28.

181. Mary Brown, "Crying Onion Café: You Can Read While You Eat," *Tucson Citizen*, October 16, 1973.
182. Rita Connelly, "Retro Restaurants," *Tucson Weekly*, February 7, 2008.
183. Jeff Smith, "At the Legendary Arroyo Café, the Regulars Show Up Early," *Tucson Citizen*, December 8, 1978.
184. Food.com, "Arroyo Café Peanut Butter Pie," http://www.food.com/recipe/arroyo-cafe-peanut-butter-pie-296301.
185. Good Earth menu; Gerdron, *Old Pueblo Review*.
186. Rebecca Cook, "Tanto Uberior," *Tucson Weekly*, June 12, 1997.
187. Sandra L. Schultz, "Greeks in Tucson," *Kiva* 45, no. 4 (Summer 1980): 285–91, http://www.jstor.org/stable/30246637; Sigesmund, "Restaurant Thrives on a Taste of the Past."
188. Wikipedia, "University of Arizona," https://en.wikipedia.org/wiki/University_of_Arizona.
189. Interview with Dr. Jim Griffith.
190. From the back of a Gentle Ben's menu, Arizona Historical Society, compiled by Margaret Neal Herndon.
191. Joe Burchell, "Speedway Widening Project Forces Big A Restaurant to Move Down Road," *Arizona Daily Star*, April 11, 1989.
192. John Bret-Harte, "The Big A, in Its New Home, Is as Good as Always," *Arizona Daily Star*, March 22, 1991.
193. Jonathan J. Higuera, "New Owner Says," *Tucson Citizen*, October 29, 1998.
194. A.J. Flick, "Bum Steer Comeback Hobbled," *Tucson Citizen*, December 11, 2007.
195. Tucson City County Council Meeting Minutes, June 9, 2007.
196. Interview with Steve Marshall, July 2015.
197. Ibid.
198. Cathalena E. Burch, "Zachery's to Close After 24 Years," Tucson.com, July 18, 2012.

Chapter 7

199. Interview with Jim "Murph" Murphy, Jeff Azersky and Marianne Baines, July 2015.
200. Interview with Doug Levy, June 2015.
201. Heather Hoch, "The Dish at Rum Runner to Close, Re-Open as Tasting Room," *Tucson Weekly*, http://www.tucsonweekly.com/TheRange/archives/2015/02/27/the-dish-at-rum-runner-to-close-re-open-as-tasting-room.
202. Cathalena Burch, "55-Year-Old Tucson Mexican Restaurant La Fuente Closes," Tucson.com, September 22, 2014.

INDEX

INDEX

INDEX

INDEX

W

Y

Z

About the Author

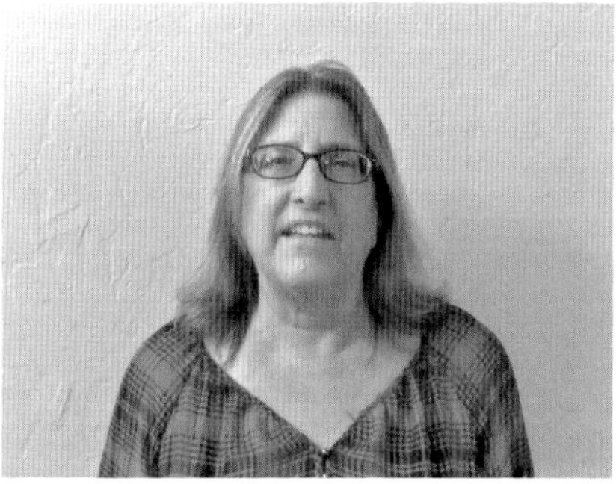

Rita Connelly first moved to Tucson in 1972 and immediately fell in love with the area. After she spent too many long winters in chilly Wisconsin, the blue skies and warm temperature of southern Arizona were like being in heaven. Her first job in Tucson was as a waitress at Ports O'Call restaurant.

In 1977, she earned her degree in secondary education from the University of Arizona and married her husband, John. It was a very good year.

The Connellys, now including daughter Riene, moved to Wisconsin for a while but then came to their senses and returned home to Tucson. Shortly after her return, she had her first of many works published. She wrote about children, health and her favorite topic, food.

In 2005, she was hired as a restaurant reviewer for the *Tucson Weekly*, where she ate and worked for ten years. She's written about the Tucson food scene for other local and national publications. She has also co-written a guidebook on Tucson. As a food writer in Tucson, she's eaten at many great restaurants, a few really bad restaurants and been a judge at hot dog, taco, salsa, margarita and chocolate competitions. Being a food writer is Rita's dream job. She gets to have fun, learn something and make a little money. Who could ask for more?